Alfarabi,

The Political Writings

Agora Editions

Editor: Thomas L. Pangle

Founding Editor: Allan Bloom

Alfarabi, *The Political Writings: "Selected Aphorisms" and Other Texts.* Translated and annotated by Charles E. Butterworth

Bolotin, David. *Plato's Dialogue on Friendship: An Interpretation of the "Lysis," with a New Translation.*

Kojève, Alexandre. *Introduction to the Reading of Hegel: Lectures on the "Phenomenology of Spirit."* Assembled by Raymond Queneau. Edited by Allan Bloom. Translated by James H. Nichols Jr.

Medieval Political Philosophy: A Sourcebook. Edited by Ralph Lerner and Muhsin Mahdi.

Plato. *Gorgias*. Translated by James H. Nichols Jr.

Plato. *Phaedrus*. Translated by James H. Nichols Jr.

Plato. *Gorgias and Phaedrus.* Translated by James H. Nichols Jr.

The Roots of Political Philosophy: Ten Forgotten Socratic Dialogues. Edited by Thomas L. Pangle.

Rousseau, Jean-Jacques. *Politics and the Arts: Letter to M. D'Alembert on the Theatre.* Translated by Allan Bloom.

ALFARABI

The Political Writings

SELECTED APHORISMS and Other Texts

TRANSLATED AND ANNOTATED BY

CHARLES E. BUTTERWORTH

Cornell University Press

ITHACA AND LONDON

First published 2001 by Cornell University Press

First printing, Cornell Paperbacks, 2004

Printed in the United States of America

LIBRARY OF CONGRESS CATALOGING-IN-PUBLICATION DATA

Farabi.
[Selections. English. 2001]
Alfarabi, the political writings : *Selected Aphorisms* and other texts / translated and annotated by Charles E. Butterworth.
p. cm.— (Agora editions)
Includes bibliographical references and index.
ISBN-13: 978-0-8014-8913-6 (pbk. : alk. paper)
ISBN-10: 0-8014-8913-X (pbk. : alk. paper)
1. Philosophy, Islamic—Early works to 1800. I. Butterworth, Charles E. II. Title.
III. Agora editions (Cornell University Press)
B753.F32 E5 2001
181'.6—dc21 00-012887

Cornell University Press strives to use environmentally responsible suppliers and materials to the fullest extent possible in the publishing of its books. Such materials include vegetable-based, low-VOC inks and acid-free papers that are recycled, totally chlorine-free, or partly composed of nonwood fibers. For further information, visit our website at www.cornellpress.cornell.edu.

Paperback printing 10 9 8 7 6 5

For
Charles "Chick" Evans Jr.,
Roland F. "Mac" McGuigan,
and Thomas Dutch,
with gratitude for their faith in
the promise of education

Contents

Preface

Widely referred to as "the second teacher," that is, second after Aristotle, Abū Naṣr Muḥammad Ibn Muḥammad Ibn Ṭarkhān Ibn Awzalagh al-Fārābī (Alfarabi) is generally heralded as having founded political philosophy within the Islamic cultural tradition. Born in about 870/256[1] in the village of Farab in Turkestan, he resided in Bukhara, Marv, Ḥarrān, Baghdad, and perhaps in Constantinople, as well as in Aleppo, Cairo, and finally Damascus, where he died in 950/339. The son of an army officer in the service of the Samanids, Alfarabi first studied Islamic jurisprudence and music in Bukhara, then moved to Marv, where he began to study logic with a Nestorian Christian monk, Yūḥannā Ibn Haylān. While in his early twenties, Alfarabi left for Baghdad, where he continued to study logic and philosophy with Ibn Ḥaylān. At the same time, he improved his grasp of Arabic by studying with the prominent philologist Ibn al-Sarrāj and is said to have followed the courses of the famous Nestorian Christian translator and student of Aristotle, Mattā Ibn Yūnus.

Around 905/293–910/298, Alfarabi left Baghdad for Byzantium (possibly even reaching Constantinople), where he remained for about eight years, studying Greek sciences and philosophy. On his return to Baghdad, he busied himself with teaching and writing until political upheavals in 942/330 forced him to seek refuge in Damascus. Two or three years later, political turmoil there drove him to Egypt, where he stayed until return-

1. That is, 870 of the Common Era and 256 of the Anno Hejirae (the year 622 C.E., when Muhammad and his followers fled from Mecca to Medina, marks the beginning of the Muslim calendar).

ing to Damascus in 948/337 or 949/338, a little over a year before his death.[2]

His writings, extraordinary in their breadth as well as in their deep learning, extend through all of the sciences and embrace every part of philosophy. Alfarabi's interest in mathematics is evidenced in commentaries on the *Elements* of Euclid and *Almagest* of Ptolemy, as well as in several writings on the history and theory of music. Indeed, his *Kitāb al-Mūsiqā al-Kabīr*, (*Large Book on Music*) may well be the most significant work in Arabic on that subject. He also wrote numerous commentaries on Aristotle's logical treatises, was knowledgeable about the Stagirite's physical writings, and is credited with an extensive commentary on the *Nicomachean Ethics* that is no longer extant. In addition to writing the accounts of Plato's and Aristotle's philosophy that form the second and third parts of the trilogy published as the first volume in this series of Alfarabi's political writings, the *Philosophy of Plato and Aristotle*, he composed a commentary on Plato's *Laws*.

As the first philosopher within the tradition of Islam to explore the challenge to traditional philosophy presented by revealed religion, especially in its claims that the Creator provides for human well-being by means of an inspired prophet legislator, Alfarabi has come to be known as the founder of Islamic political philosophy. In the first part of the *Philosophy of Plato and Aristotle*—that is, in the *Attainment of Happiness*—he seeks to pinpoint the common concerns that link Islam and its revealed law with pagan philosophy in its highest form—namely, the writings of Plato and Aristotle. That effort finds an echo in the *Selected Aphorisms*, the first writing presented in this volume, in two ways. First, the opening words of the treatise indicate that Alfarabi draws from what the ancients—that is, Plato and Aristotle—have to say about governing, but governing with a view to a particular purpose. For him, the goal is to govern cities so that they become prosperous and the lives of their citizens are improved—this in the sense that they be led toward happiness. Second, the overlap between this work and the *Philosophy of Plato and Aristotle*, especially the *Attainment of Happiness*, indicated by these words is made even more explicit toward the end of the *Selected Aphorisms*. Indeed, a long passage in aphorism 94 paraphrases sections 11–20 of the *Attainment of Happiness*.

2. For the preceding biographical observations, see Muhsin S. Mahdi, "Al-Fārābī," in *Dictionary of Scientific Biography*, ed. C. C. Gillispie (New York: Charles Scribner, 1971), vol. 4, pp. 523–26; and "Al-Fārābī's Imperfect State," in *Journal of the American Oriental Society* 110, no.4 (1990): 712–13.

Yet Alfarabi seems always alert to the difficulties religion and revealed law pose for the older approach to politics. In the fifth chapter of the *Enumeration of the Sciences,* for example, he sets forth two accounts of the old political science. Both presuppose the validity of the traditional separation between the practical and the theoretical sciences, but neither is adequate for the radically new situation created by the appearance of revealed religion. The two accounts explain in detail the actions and ways of life required for sound political rule to flourish, but are utterly silent about opinions—especially the kind of theoretical opinions that have been set forth in the now dominant religion—and thus are unable, given this religion's prevalence, to point to the kind of rulership needed. Nor can either speak about the opinions or actions addressed by the jurisprudence and theology of revealed religion. These tasks require a political science that both combines theoretical and practical sciences along with prudence and shows how they are to be ordered in the soul of the ruler.

Such a view of political science is presented in the *Book of Religion.* It is a political science that is a part of philosophy. Yet even as Alfarabi offers this redemptive vision of political science, he suggests that religion and revelation must also be put into perspective or considered anew and then goes about explaining religion in such a manner that its theoretical and practical subordination to philosophy becomes manifest. Alfarabi's account of this subordination makes it seem perfectly reasonable—so reasonable that the limitations thereby placed on dialectical theology and jurisprudence appear to follow necessarily from it.

To this explanation of the way Alfarabi elaborates the relationship between the philosophy of the ancients and the new revelation, one might object that it relies too much on a presumption of harmony and agreement between Plato and Aristotle on these matters. We know, however, that the two differed about many minor and not-so-minor questions. This issue is addressed in the last work presented in this volume, the highly enigmatic *Harmonization of the Two Opinions of the Two Sages, Plato the Divine and Aristotle.* Here Alfarabi, desirous of putting an end to the disputes and discord among his contemporaries about the disagreement they claim to discern between "the two eminent and distinguished sages, Plato and Aristotle," sets out to show that their opinions are in agreement, to "remove doubt and suspicion from the hearts of those who look into their books," and to "explain the places of uncertainty and the sources of doubt in their treatises." These goals, set forth in the opening words of the treatise, are surely most appealing. But do they not too readily discount or ignore simple facts manifest to any student of Plato and Aristotle? Precisely for that reason, the reader must look again at Alfarabi's final observation as he begins this treatise: he deems the attempt to show the agreement or harmonization between these two philosophers' teachings to be of the utmost importance and, in addition, a most beneficial matter "to expound upon and elucidate." Stated differently, whether such agreement exists in fact or not, concern for the commonweal prompts Alfarabi to seek for a means of bringing something like agreement to light.

Such are the general features of and linkages between the texts before us. Each has translated anew for this volume, and each translation relies either on a text newly edited or on the revision of an older edition. To the extent consonant with readable English, Arabic terms have been rendered consistently by the same English word. Similarly, every effort has been made to ensure that once an English word is used for a particular Arabic term, it is subsequently used only for that term. The goal is to reproduce in faithful and readable English the argument of these Arabic texts in a manner that captures their texture and style and also communicates the nuances and variety of Alfarabi's expression. To this end, notes sometimes point to particular problems in a passage or to the fact that considerations of style or sense have made it necessary to render an important term differently. An English–Arabic and Arabic–English glossary has been placed at the end of the volume to provide the interested reader with the possibility of investigating how particular words have been translated.

The translations presented here have benefited from the kindly suggestions of many readers, especially the students in undergraduate and graduate seminars at the University of Maryland, Georgetown University, and Harvard University, who wrestled valiantly with the complexities of Alfarabi's thought and expression. May they and all those fellow scholars who have read these translations with such care, pondered over my attempts to render Alfarabi's teaching in something approaching conventional English, and helped me present it more precisely or perhaps more elegantly, find here my warmest expressions of gratitude. Special thanks are due also to five individuals, each of whom contributed massively to this project. First, as all students of Alfarabi know so well, Professor Muhsin Mahdi discovered many of the manuscripts on which these translations are based and prepared the excellent critical edition of the *Book of Religion*. In addition, I have benefited greatly from his sound advice on how to resolve particular textual problems. Professor Fauzi M. Najjar's sterling editions of *Selected Aphorisms* and *Harmonization* have proved to be especially helpful, as have his initiative and assistance in translating the latter for this book. Every translator should be so fortunate to have a reader like Miriam Galston, who allows almost nothing to pass unquestioned, especially not infelicities of expression that admit of remedy. If these translations now have anything approaching literary appeal or elegance and some greater accuracy, it is largely due to her painstaking reading of the final manuscript and to her constant probing; for that precious gift of time and effort, my gratitude is boundless. I was also fortunate to have in Thomas Pangle a series editor willing to read each translation with great care, suggest ever so tactfully how awkward formulations might be better phrased, and query passages whose opacity had eluded me. Rima Pavalko's careful eye for details and gracious assistance with editorial tasks have been invaluable. To each of these benefactors, I express my deepest thanks and hope that this end product will seem worthy of their efforts. Finally, it is a great pleasure to acknowledge the support of the Earhart Foundation.

Selected Aphorisms

The translation

This translation is based on the text of the Selected Aphorisms edited by Fauzi M. Najjar just over a quarter of a century ago.[1] Najjar's edition was intended to expand upon, correct, and generally improve the edition and translation published by D. M. Dunlop a decade earlier.[2] It was primarily Muhsin Mahdi's discovery in Turkey of an older and more reliable manuscript of this work that prompted the new edition. This manuscript, from the Diyarbekir Central Library (no. 1970), had not been known to Dunlop and offered better readings of key passages as well as a more complete text. In addition, Mahdi discovered another Turkish manuscript unknown to Dunlop—the Istanbul Millet Library, Feyzullah, no. 1279. Though it was not much more reliable than the two manuscripts on which Dunlop had based his work (the Chester Beatty, no. 3714; and Bodleian, Hunt., no. 307), Najjar's acquisition of copies of two other manuscripts unknown to Dunlop (the University of Teheran, Central Library, Mishkāt, no. 250, and the University of Teheran, Faculty of Divinity, Ilāhiyyāt, no. 695) allowed him to improve considerably upon Dunlop's edition. These improvements appear throughout the text, but are especially evident in the new aphorisms (3, 15, 23, and 40) and the additional sentences in aphorisms 6,

1. See *Abū Naṣr al-Fārābī, Fuṣūl Muntazaʿa,* (Selected Aphorisms), edited, with an introduction and notes, by Fauzi M. Najjar (Beirut: Dār al-Mashriq, 1971).

2. See *Al-Fārābi: Fuṣūl al-Madanī, Aphorisms of the Statesman,* edited with an English translation, introduction and notes, by D. M. Dunlop (Cambridge: Cambridge University Press, 1961).

8, and 26 (corresponding to Dunlop's 5, 7, and 23). Again, in aphorisms 68–87, where Dunlop had to rely solely on the Chester Beatty source, Najjar's richer manuscript base offered far better textual readings and clarified many problems Dunlop had not been able to resolve.

The numbering of the aphorisms in the present translation corresponds to Najjar's edition, but the section titles and other material found within square brackets have been added by me. Some of these divisions are supported by marginal notations found in the Diyarbekir and University of Teheran Central Library manuscripts. Still, Dunlop's erroneous division of the text into two parts (aphorisms 1–65 and 66–96) on the basis of a marginal note in the Chester Beatty manuscript shows that such decisions cannot be reached on the basis of scribal marginalia alone, but must also be consonant with the sense of the argument.[3] Also of my doing is the sentence punctuation and paragraph divisions within the aphorisms. The numbers within square brackets refer to the pages of Najjar's Arabic text. With these additions, as with the notes, my primary goal has been to make it easier for the reader to seize and follow Alfarabi's argument.

The same goal guides this translation. Years of using Dunlop's translation with students who do not read Arabic showed that it would not be sufficient merely to insert Najjar's new aphorisms and otherwise lightly touch up his version. Rather, it had become clear that a technically rigorous rendering of the text was needed. For example, in aphorism 57, Dunlop renders the term *al-madīna al-fāḍila*, not as "the virtuous city" (which corresponds to the context and its discussion of virtue) but as "the ideal city." In aphorism 2, where Alfarabi contrasts noble actions (*al-af ʿāl al-jamīla*) with base actions (*al-af ʿāl al-qabīḥa*), a contrast perfectly in keeping with the other one he is making between virtue and vice, Dunlop translates these as "fair actions" and "ugly actions," thereby leaving the reader to wonder what Alfarabi is talking about. In keeping with this lack of rigor is Dunlop's tendency to use different English terms for the same Arabic terms and the same English term to translate different Arabic ones, a practice that deprives the reader of learning anything about Alfarabi's philosophic or political vocabulary.

To be sure, the contrary practice I have adopted sometimes obliges the reader to pause and puzzle out certain passages. The attempt to render Arabic terms consistently with the same English ones does not always lend

3. See Muhsin Mahdi, "Review of *Al-Fārābī: Fuṣūl al-Madanī, Aphorisms of the Statesman*," *Journal of Near Eastern Studies* 23 (1964): 140–43.

itself to seamless, fluid prose. It should come as no surprise that particularly when he is engaged in discussions of difficult questions, as when he is explaining wisdom (aph. 37), Alfarabi's Arabic prose is equally strained. The extremes to be avoided in translation seem to be the excessive pedantry or desire for precision that creates confusion where none exists and the insufficient attentiveness that leads to smoothing over just those difficulties that one ought not remove. Though awareness of them offers no immunity, it is surely a better portent for a translation than nescience.

The title of the work

Only one of the known manuscripts—namely, the "Book of the Aphorisms of the Statesman, by Abū Naṣr al-Fārābī"—offers a title. It is also one of the latest and least reliable manuscripts, the Bodleian. Moreover, no medieval bibliographic source attributes a book with this title to Alfarabi; nor does the famous nineteenth century historian of medieval Islamic and Jewish philosophy, Moritz Steinschneider, ever refer to it by this name. He, like Najjar, looks back to those traditional sources as well as to the way the work is identified in the first few lines of the other manuscripts and opts for the appellation "The Selected Aphorisms"; in doing so, Steinschneider departs only minutely from the other title traditionally assigned the work, the one Najjar opts for—"Selected Aphorisms."[4]

Najjar relies principally upon the Diyarbekir manuscript to establish this title. With minor variations, the first few lines of this manuscript and three of the other five manuscripts read:

> Selected aphorisms that comprise the roots of many of the sayings of the Ancients concerning that by which cities ought to be governed and made prosperous, the ways of life of their inhabitants improved, and they be led toward happiness.

The emphasis here is thus on the partial character of the treatise: it contains selected aphorisms that encompass the foundations, principles, or grounds of several—that is, not all—of the sayings of the ancients. Moreover, those sayings are limited to political subjects, especially ones relating to rule. Only in the two Teheran manuscripts is a reading substantially different from this prefatory passage to be found. Because it places greater

4. See Najjar, pp. 10–13 and notes.

stress upon human virtue than on political order and thereby suggests a different orientation to the work, it is worth citing in full:

> These are the sentences and aphorisms chosen from the science of morals [and] comprise: acquiring the virtues of the human soul, avoiding its vices, moving the human being himself from his bad habits to fine habits, making firm the virtuous city, and making firm the household and the rulership over its inhabitants. They are all brought together in this epistle.[5]

Moreover, in both these manuscripts the work is identified as an epistle (*risāla*). Such differences notwithstanding, insofar as both versions provide a summary preview of the argument to come, they may well be nothing more than attempts on the part of industrious scribes to offer readers a preliminary synopsis of the work.

In translating the term *fuṣūl* (sing. *faṣl*) as "aphorisms" here, I do no more than follow in the steps of the first editor and translator—Dunlop—just as the second editor—Najjar—and most other scholars have done. Yet Dunlop's recourse to Maimonides in order to urge that aphorisms are necessarily incomplete or fall short of a fully scientific explanation seems unwarranted.[6] Nor, pithy as they are, is anything to be gained by conjecturing that Alfarabi understands *fuṣūl* to mean "aphorisms" in the sense Nietzsche ascribes to the term almost a millennium later.[7] The matter is much more straightforward: we need only note how "aphorism," derived from the Greek *aphorizein* ("to mark off" or "to determine"), is aptly captured by the Arabic *faṣl* and understand the English term in light of its Greek origin. Indeed, since Alfarabi at no point indicates why he calls the divisions of this work *fuṣūl*, he may mean nothing more by the term than "sections" or some other form of textual break. Still, given the shortness of many of the *fuṣūl*, there is no good reason to call them "chapters."

The structure of the work

The work itself consists of 96 aphorisms. The four additional and contested aphorisms, found only in the most recent and least reliable of the

5. See Najjar, p. 23 note 2. In parentheses, Najjar adds "five chapters" (*khamsat abwāb*) after "epistle," but the link with the rest of the note is not evident.

6. See Dunlop, p. 10.

7. See Friedrich Nietzsche, *Zur Genealogie der Moral* (Towards a genealogy of morals) Preface, no. 8; and also *Morgenröte* (Daybreak), no. 454.

six manuscripts, are sufficiently problematic that it is best to set them apart. In the *Selected Aphorisms,* Alfarabi begins with, then develops, a comparison between the health of the soul and that of the body. That is, somewhat abruptly, he starts his exposition by defining the health of each and then explains how the health of the more important of the two—that of the soul—may be obtained and its sickness repulsed. The first word of the *Selected Aphorisms* is simply "soul," while the last is "virtue." In the 96 aphorisms occurring between these two words, Alfarabi first enters upon a detailed examination of the soul, then provides an account and justification of the well-ordered political regime that the soul needs in order to attain its perfection. At no point in the treatise or epistle does he speak of prophecy or of the prophet or legislator. The terms are not even evoked. He is equally silent with respect to the philosopher and mentions "philosophy" only twice, both in the antepenultimate aphorism 94—the same aphorism in which he mentions, for the only time, the word "revelation." On the other hand, Alfarabi speaks constantly throughout these aphorisms of the statesman (*madanī*) and of the king.

The "Ancients" referred to in the few lines preceding the first aphorism are, of course, none other than Plato and Aristotle. Alfarabi calls upon them in this work to identify the political order that will bring about human happiness. The individual who succeeds in understanding how a political community can be well-ordered—whether this person is a statesman or a king—will do for the citizens what the physician does for individual sick persons and will accomplish for the citizens who follow his rules what the prophet accomplishes for those who follow his. Nonetheless, to attain such an understanding, one must first be fully acquainted with the soul as well as with political life. More precisely, the virtuous political regime is the one in which the souls of all the inhabitants are as healthy as possible: "the one who cures souls is the statesman, and he is also called the king" (aph. 4).

This is why such a patently political treatise contains two long discussions of the soul. One, very reminiscent of what is found in the *Nicomachean Ethics,* explains all the faculties of the soul except for the theoretical part of the rational faculty (aphs. 6–21). The other analyzes this theoretical part as well as its companion, the practical part, by discussing the intellectual virtues (aphs. 33–56). In addition, there is an investigation of the sound and erroneous opinions with respect to the principles of being and happiness (aphs. 68–87). These three groups of aphorisms constitute a little less than two-thirds of the treatise. Void of formal structure or divisions, the treatise unfolds in such a manner that each moral discussion is preceded and followed by other groups of aphorisms that go more deeply into its political teaching.

Thus, the discussion of the soul in general is preceded by a series of analogies between the soul and the body as well as between the soul and the body politic (aphs. 1–5) and followed first by a discussion devoted to domestic political economy (aphs. 22–29) and then by an inquiry into the king in truth (aphs. 30–32). The second discussion of the soul, preceded by these three aphorisms, is followed by an inquiry into the virtuous city (aphs. 57–67). This in turn precedes the investigation of sound and erroneous opinions, itself followed by the account of the virtuous regime (aphs. 88–96). Subsequent to each moral digression, the tone of the discussion seems to become more elevated, almost as though the moral teaching were the driving force for the political teaching of the treatise or were at least giving it direction.

Here, then, is the schematic structure of the treatise or epistle as I understand it:

A. ANALOGIES BETWEEN THE SOUL AND THE BODY AND THEN BETWEEN THE SOUL AND THE BODY POLITIC (aphs.1–5)
B. THE HUMAN SOUL, ITS VIRTUES AND VICES (aphs. 6–21)
C. HOUSEHOLDS, DWELLINGS, AND CITIES (aphs. 22–29)
D. ON THE KING IN TRUTH (aphs. 30–32)
E. THE INTELLECTUAL VIRTUES (aphs. 33–56)
F. THE VIRTUOUS CITY (aphs. 57–67)
G. THE DIVISIONS OF BEING AND THE STATUS OF HAPPINESS: SOUND VS. ERRONEOUS OPINIONS (aphs. 68–87)
H. THE VIRTUOUS REGIME (aphs. 88–96)
I. THE DOUBTFUL APHORISMS (aphs. 97–100)

Such an explanation of the general structure of Alfarabi's *Selected Aphorisms* and identification of its major themes raise at least two questions. First, what do aphorisms 22–29 and 30–32 bring to the general exposition that warrants their interrupting Alfarabi's explanation of the human soul and its faculties (aphs. 6–21 and 33–56)? Or, differently stated, why can Alfarabi not provide a full account of the soul's faculties—especially of its intellectual faculty—before having discussed the way human beings live together and a particular kind of monarch? Clearly, his discussion of the deeper significance behind seemingly basic practical arrangements to facilitate life in community and of the qualities obviously desirable in one identified as the best possible ruler prepares—indeed, it presupposes—a fuller account of the soul. That is, Alfarabi's exposition points to the limitations of moral virtue. For life in common and, even more, for the best kind of political rule, human beings need more than moderation and courage.

The second question arising from attention to the structure of this work has to do with the topics of aphorisms 68–87. Once the human soul has been fully explained—that is, once its moral and intellectual excellences have been identified and described in detail—Alfarabi focuses on providing for the soul in a proper political order. So what prompts him to pause in the middle of that discussion and turn to questions having to do with physical science as well as with metaphysics or even theology? This question, too, admits of a different formulation: why is it necessary to distinguish the sound opinions about the principles of being and the status of happiness from the erroneous ones before moving from a discussion of a particular form of virtuous political community, the city, to the virtuous regime in general? It almost seems that the virtuous city is so particular and so dependent on a series of fortuitous circumstances coming about as to absolve Alfarabi from providing a full-blown account of being and happiness when his attention is focused on that city. With respect to it, a merely persuasive account of such matters will suffice. When the broader political entity encompassed by the term regime is being investigated, however, something more is needed. Something more is needed because what can be gained in the regime, for the ruler as well as for the ruled, far surpasses what can be gained in the city. The distinction between the two turns not on their relative size—not, that is, on the notion that the regime is larger insofar as it encompasses a number of cities—but on the greater virtue and greater happiness to which both ruler and ruled can aspire in the virtuous regime (aph. 89). Here alone, or so it seems, can ruler and ruled aspire to completing themselves as human beings.

In this sense, the title formerly ascribed to the work, *Aphorisms of the Statesman*, is almost more appropriate than the one by which it is presented here, *Selected Aphorisms*. These are aphorisms that tell the would-be statesman precisely the kind of things he needs to know in order to rule. They answer, with concision, the questions he might raise about the moral and intellectual virtues, about the way people live together, and so forth. What is more, these aphorisms draw upon the wisdom of Plato and Aristotle—as much the one as the other—in order to answer such questions.

The same line of reasoning explains another characteristic of this work: the fundamental or basic character of its teaching—its appearance as something like a primer for politics. Alfarabi posits in this work the fundamentals with respect to the soul, the city, and ruling. Drawing on Aristotle without saying so, he provides an excellent summary of the key points of the *Nicomachean Ethics* with respect to the moral virtues, the distinction between virtue and self-restraint, and the intellectual virtues. Then, drawing on Plato without saying so, he provides a kind of summary of the *Republic* to explain the idea of political justice and the basic distribution of duties in the virtuous city. He also explains what opinions one should hold about the soul and its faculties, the life to come, the principles of being, ultimate happiness, and similar matters. As a result, it becomes perfectly patent here that good practice presupposes correct understanding or that knowledge is virtue.

Selected Aphorisms

[23] Selected aphorisms that comprise the roots of many of the sayings of the Ancients concerning that by which cities ought to be governed and made prosperous, the ways of life of their inhabitants improved, and they be led toward happiness.

[A. ANALOGIES BETWEEN THE SOUL AND THE BODY AND THEN BETWEEN THE SOUL AND THE BODY POLITIC.]

1. Aphorism. The soul has health and sickness just as the body has health and sickness. The health of the soul is for its traits and the traits of its parts to be traits by which it can always do good things, fine things, and noble actions. Its sickness is for its traits and the traits of its parts to be traits by which it always does evil things, wicked things, and base actions. The health of the body is for its traits and the traits of its parts to be traits by which the soul does its actions in the most complete and perfect way, whether those [24] actions that come about by means of the body or its parts are good ones or evil ones. Its sickness is for its traits and the traits of its parts to be traits by which the soul does not do its actions that come about by means of the body or its parts, or does them in a more diminished manner than it ought or not[1] as was its wont to do them.

1. Reading *aw lā*, for sense, rather than *awwalan* ("first").

2. Aphorism. The traits of the soul by which a human being does good things and noble actions are virtues. Those by which he does evil things and base actions are vices, defects, and villainies.

3. Aphorism. Just as the health of the body is an equilibrium of its temperament and its sickness is a deviation from equilibrium, so, too, are the health of the city and its uprightness an equilibrium of the moral habits of its inhabitants and its sickness a disparity found in their moral habits. When the body deviates from equilibrium in its temperament, the one who brings it back to equilibrium and preserves it there is the physician. So, too, when the city deviates from equilibrium with respect to the moral habits of its inhabitants, the one who brings it back to uprightness and preserves it there is the statesman. So the statesman and physician have their two actions in common and differ with respect to the two subjects of their two arts. For the subject of the former is souls and the subject of the latter, bodies. And just as the soul is more eminent than the body, so, too, is the statesman more eminent than the physician.

4. Aphorism. The one who cures bodies is the physician; and the one who cures souls is the statesman, and he is also called the king. However, the intention of the physician in curing bodies is not to make its traits such that the soul does good things or wicked ones by means of them. Rather, he intends only to make its traits such that by means of them the actions of the soul coming about by means of the body and its parts are [25] more perfect, whether those actions are wicked things or fine ones.

The physician who cures the body does so only to improve a human being's strength, regardless of whether he uses that improved[2] strength in fine things or wicked ones. The one who cures the eye intends thereby only to improve sight, regardless of whether he uses that in what he ought and becomes fine or in what he ought not and becomes base. Therefore, to look into the health of the body and its sickness from this perspective is not up to the physician insofar as he is a physician, but up to the statesman and the king. Indeed, the statesman by means of the political art and the king by means of the art of kingship determine where it ought to be done, with respect to whom it ought to be done and with respect to whom not done, and what sort of health bodies ought to be provided with and what sort they ought not to be provided with.

2. Literally, "excellent" (*al-jayyid*).

Therefore, the case of the kingly and the political art[3] with respect to the rest of the arts in cities is that of the master builder with respect to the builders. For the rest of the arts in cities are carried out and practiced only so as to complete by means of them the purpose of the political art and the kingly art,[4] just as the ruling art among the arts of the builders uses the rest of them in order to complete its intention by means of them.

5. Aphorism. The physician who cures bodies needs to be cognizant[5] of [26] the body in its entirety and of the parts of the body, of what sicknesses occur to the whole of the body and to each one of its parts, from what they occur, from how much of a thing, of the way to make them cease, and of the traits that when attained by the body and its parts make the actions coming about in the body perfect and complete. Likewise, the statesman and the king who cure souls need to be cognizant of the soul in its entirety and of its parts, of what defects and vices occur to it and to each one of its parts, from what they occur, from how much of a thing, of the traits of the soul by which a human does good things and how many they are, of the way to make the vices of the inhabitants of cities cease, of the devices to establish these traits in the souls of the citizens, and of the way of governing so as to preserve these traits among them so that they do not cease. And yet[6] he ought to be cognizant of only as much about the soul as is needed in his art just as the physician needs to be cognizant of only as much about the body as is needed in his art, and the carpenter with respect to wood or the smith with respect to iron only as much as is needed in his art.

[B. THE HUMAN SOUL, ITS VIRTUES AND VICES]

6. Aphorism. Some bodies are artificial and some are natural. The artificial are like a couch, a sword, glass, and similar things. The natural are

3. Reading *ṣināʿat al-malik wa al-madaniyya,* for sense, rather than *ṣināʿat al-mulk wa al-madīna* ("the art of kingship and of the city").

4. Reading wa *bi-ṣināʿat al-malik,* for sense, rather than *wa bi-ṣināʿat al-mulk* ("the art of kingship").

5. The term is *ʿarafa;* here and in what follows I translate it and its substantive, *maʿrifa,* as "to be cognizant of" or "to recognize," and "cognizance," in order to distinguish them from *ʿalima and ʿilm,* which I translate as "to know," and "science" or "knowledge." The goal of such a distinction is to preserve the difference between *gignōskein* and *epistasthai* that these terms seem to reflect.

6. Reading *wa lākin innamā,* with all the manuscripts except the Diyarbekir.

like human beings and the rest of the animals. Every one of them is joined together from two things, one of which is matter and the other form. The matter of an artificial body [27] is like the wood of a couch, and the form is like the shape of the couch, namely, its being square, round, or otherwise. Matter is potentially a couch; by means of the form it becomes a couch in actuality. The matter of a natural body is its elements, and the form is that by which each becomes what it is. Genera are similar to matters, and differentiae are similar to forms.[7]

7. Aphorism. There are five major parts and faculties of the soul: the nutritive; the sense perceptive; the imaginative; the appetitive; and the rational.

[a] In general, the nutritive is the one that carries out a certain action upon, by means of, or from, nutriment.

There are three types of nutriment: primary, intermediate, and final. The primary is like bread, flesh, and all that has not yet begun to be digested. The final is that which has been completely digested until it has become similar to the member that is nourished by it: if the member is flesh, then insofar as that nutriment becomes flesh; and if it is bone, then [by becoming] bone. The intermediate is of two types. One is that which is cooked in the stomach and intestines until it has become prepared for blood to come from it, and the second is blood.

Of the nutritive there are the digestive, growing, procreative, attracting, retentive, distinguishing, and expelling faculties. The more appropriate way to speak about[8] the nutritive is that it is what simmers the blood, reaching each and every member until it becomes similar to that member.

The digestive is what simmers the primary nutriment in the stomach and intestines until it becomes prepared for blood to come from it, then what cooks this preparation—in the liver, for example—until it becomes blood.

The growing is what, by means of nutriment, [28] increases the quantity of the member in all its dimensions during development until each member reaches its ultimate possible size.

The procreative is what—from the surplus of nutriment close to the

7. Particular beings fit into broader classes such as body, self-nourishing, animal, and human. A genus is the more general class that encompasses the classes called species. Thus, the species of human being, donkey, and horse all fall under the genera of animal, self-nourishing, and the ultimate genus of body. To distinguish one species in a genus from another species in the same genus, recourse is had to the differentia, as when the human being is distinguished from the donkey and the horse by means of reason.

8. Literally, "the more truthful way to call" (*wa ạhaqq mā yusammī*).

final, namely, the blood—makes another body similar in kind to the body from whose nutriment the surplus overflowed. These are of two sorts. One gives matter to what is procreated, namely, the female; and the other gives it form, namely, the male. From these two, it comes to be that an animal coming into being from another is similar to it in kind.

The attracting is what attracts the nutriment from place to place until it arrives at the body being nourished so as to come into contact with it and blend with it.

The retentive is what preserves nutriment in the vessel of the body it has reached.

The distinguishing is what distinguishes the surplus amounts of nutriment and the sorts of nutriment, then distributes to every member what resembles it.

The expelling is what expels the sorts of surplus amounts of nutriment from place to place.

[b] The sense perceptive faculty is the one that perceives by means of one of the five senses of which everyone is cognizant.

[c] The imaginative is the one that preserves the traces of sense perceptions after their absence from the contact of the senses, brings about different combinations of some with others, and separates some from others in many different ways—some of these being accurate and some being false. And this occurs both in waking and in sleep. This and the nutritive, apart from the rest of the faculties, may be active in sleep.

[d] The appetitive faculty is that by which the appetition of an animal for something comes about and by which there is longing for [29] something, loathing for it, seeking and fleeing, preference and avoidance, anger and contentedness, fear and boldness, harshness and compassion, love and hatred,[9] passion, desire, and the rest of the accidents of the soul. The tools of this faculty are all of the faculties by which the movements of every one of the members and of the body in its entirety are facilitated, such as the faculty of the hands for strength, the legs for walking, and other members.

[e] The rational faculty is the one by which a human being intellects, carries out deliberation, acquires the sciences and arts, and distinguishes between noble and base actions. Of it, there is practical and theoretical. Of the practical, some involves skill and some calculation.

9. There is no necessity that the affections enumerated here—that is, seeking and fleeing, preference and avoidance, anger and contentedness, fear and boldness, harshness and compassion, love and hatred—be read as pairs. The text permits reading them as individual affections.

The theoretical is that by which a human being has knowledge of the beings that are not such that we can act upon them or alter them from one condition to another. Three, for example, is an odd number and four an even number. It is not possible for us to alter three so that it becomes even while remaining three, nor four so that it becomes odd while remaining four, though it is possible for us to alter wood so that it becomes round after having been square while remaining wood in both conditions.

The practical is what distinguishes the things such that we act upon them and alter them from one condition to another. What involves skill or art is that by which crafts such as carpentry, farming, medicine, and sailing are acquired. What involves calculation is that by which we deliberate[10] about [30] something we want to do when we want to do it, whether it is possible to do or not and, if it is possible, how that ought to be done.

8. Aphorism. The virtues are of two sorts, moral and rational. The rational are the virtues of the rational part such as wisdom, intellect, cleverness, quick-wittedness, and excellent understanding.[11] The moral are the virtues of the appetitive part such as moderation, courage, liberality, and justice. Likewise, the vices are divided in this manner and are, within the compass of each of the divisions, the contraries of these that have been enumerated and of their purposes.

9. Aphorism. The moral virtues and vices are attained and established in the soul only by repeating the actions coming about from that moral habit many times over a certain time [period] and accustoming ourselves to them. If those actions are good things, what we attain is virtue; and if they are evil things, what we attain is vice. It is like this with arts such as writing. For by our repeating the actions of writing many times and accustoming ourselves to them, we attain the art of writing and it becomes established in us. If the actions of writing we repeat and accustom ourselves to are bad, wretched[12] writing is established in us; and if they are excellent actions, excellent writing is established in us. [31]

10. Reading *nurawwī*, with the Chester Beatty and Feyzullah manuscripts, rather than *yurawwī* ("one deliberates") or *yurawway* ("it is deliberated"), with Najjar and the Diyarbekir manuscript.

11. These virtues will be discussed more fully below in aphorisms 33–49.

12. Literally, "wicked" (*sū'*).

10. Aphorism. It is not possible for a human being to be endowed by nature from the outset possessing virtue or vice, just as it is not possible for a human being to be endowed by nature as a weaver or a scribe. But it is possible for one to be endowed by nature disposed for virtuous or vicious actions in that such actions are easier for him than other actions, just as it is possible to be disposed by nature for the actions of writing or of another art in that its actions are easier for him than other actions. Thus from the outset he is moved to do what is by nature easier for him when he is not prompted to its contrary by some prompting from outside. That natural disposition is not said to be a virtue, just as the natural disposition for the actions of an art is not said to be an art.

But when there is a natural disposition for virtuous actions and those actions are repeated,[13] a trait is established by custom in the soul, and those very actions issue forth from it, then the trait established by custom is what is said to be a virtue. The natural trait is not called a virtue nor a defect even if one and the same action issues forth from it. [32] The natural ones have no name. If someone calls them a virtue or a defect, he calls them so only due to homonymity, not due to the meaning of the latter being the meaning of the former. Those [actions] due to custom are those for which a human being is praised or blamed, whereas a human being is not praised or blamed for the others.

11. Aphorism. It is difficult and unusual that someone exist who is completely disposed by nature for all the virtues, moral and rational, just as it is difficult that someone exist who is naturally disposed for all the arts. Similarly, it is difficult and unusual that someone exist who is naturally disposed for all the evil actions. Yet neither matter is impossible. More often, everyone is disposed for a certain virtue, virtues of a definite number, a certain art, or a definite number of certain arts. So this [individual] is disposed for one thing,[14] another disposed for another thing, and a third [individual] disposed for some third virtue or art.

12. Aphorism. When to the natural traits and dispositions for virtue or vice are added the moral habits resembling them and they are established

13. Omitting *wa uʿtīdat* ("and are made customary"), with the University of Teheran, Faculty of Divinity manuscript.

14. Reading *naḥwa shai' awwal* (literally, "for a first thing"), with the Chester Beatty and Feyzullah manuscripts, rather than *naḥwa dhā* ("for that"), with Najjar and the other manuscripts.

by custom, that human being is [33] as complete as can be with respect to that thing. It is difficult for a trait established in a human being to be removed, whether it be good or evil.

When at some time someone exists who is completely disposed by nature for all of the virtues and they are then established in him by custom, this human being surpasses in virtue the virtues found among most people to the point that he almost goes beyond the human virtues to a higher class of humanity. The Ancients used to call this human being divine. The one contrary to him and disposed to all of the evil actions, in whom the traits of those evils are established by custom, they almost place beyond the human evils to what is even more evil. They have no name for the excess of his evil and sometimes call him a beast and similar names.

It is rare for these two extremes to be found in people. When the first exists, he is of a higher rank according to them than being a statesman who serves one of[15] the cities. Rather he governs all cities and is the king in truth. When the second happens to exist, he does not rule any city at all, nor does he serve it; rather, he goes away from all cities.

13. Aphorism. Some natural traits and dispositions for virtue or vice may be completely removed or altered by custom so that contrary traits are established in the soul in their stead. [34] With others, their power is broken, weakened, and made defective without their being completely removed. And others are not removed or altered, nor is their power made defective; but they are resisted by endurance, by restraining the soul from their actions, by contending, and by withstanding until a human being always does the contraries of their actions. Similarly, when bad moral habits are established in the soul by custom, they are also divided in this manner.

14. Aphorism. There is a difference between the one who is self-restrained and the one who is virtuous.

That is, even if the one who is self-restrained does virtuous actions, he does good things while having a passion and a longing for evil. He contends against his passion and resists what his trait and his yearning inspire him to do. He does good things and is irritated at doing them. The

15. Adding *madīna min* before *al-mudun*, with the Feyzullah manuscript.

one who is virtuous follows what his trait and his yearning inspire him to do. He carries out good things while having a passion and a longing for them, and he is not irritated at [doing] them; rather, he takes pleasure in them.

That is like the difference between the one who endures the severe pain he encounters and the one who is not pained and does not feel pain. Similarly, there is the one who is moderate and the one who is self-restrained. The one who is moderate [35] does only what traditional law[16] requires of him with respect to eating, drinking, and sexual intercourse, without having a desire or a longing for what is in addition to what the traditional law requires. The longing of the one who is self-restrained is excessive with respect to these things and other than what the traditional law requires. He does the actions of the traditional law, while his yearning is for their contrary. Yet the one who is self-restrained may take the place of the one who is virtuous with respect to many matters.

15. Aphorism. The person of praiseworthy moral [virtue] whose soul inclines to no vice at all differs from the self-restrained person with respect to the excellence to which each lays claim. If the governor of cities possesses praiseworthy morals and his praiseworthy acts are states of character, then he is more excellent than if he were self-restrained. Whereas if the citizen and the one by whom cities are made prosperous restrains himself in accordance with what the nomos[17] requires, he is more virtuous than if his virtues were natural.

The cause for that is that the self-restrained person and the one who adheres to the nomos lay claim to the virtue of struggle. If he lapses as a citizen rather than as a ruler, the rulers will set him straight; his crime and corruption do not go beyond him. The righteousness of the ruler, however, is shared by the inhabitants of his kingdom. So if he lapses at all, his corruption extends to many besides him. His virtues must be natural and be states of character, and a sufficient reward for him is what he erects in those whom he sets straight.

16. Aphorism. Evils are made to cease in cities either by virtues that are established in the souls of the people or by their becoming self-restrained.

16. The term is *sunna*.
17. The term is *nāmūs*.

Any human being whose evil cannot be made to cease by a virtue being established in his soul or by self-restraint is to be put outside of cities.

17. Aphorism. It is difficult, nay impossible, for a human being to be so endowed as [36] to be disposed for actions, then to be unable to do the contraries of those actions. Yet any human being endowed with a trait and disposition for virtuous or vicious actions is able to resist and to do the action arising from the contrary of that disposition. But that is difficult for him until it becomes facilitated and easy through custom, as is the case with what is established by custom. For abandoning what has become customary and doing its contrary is possible but difficult until it also becomes customary.

18. Aphorism. Actions that are good are equilibrated actions intermediate between two extremes, both of which are evil: one being an excess, and the other a deficiency. Similarly, virtues are traits of the soul and states intermediate between two traits both of which are vices, one of which is greater and the other lesser—like moderation, for it is intermediate between avidity and insensibility to pleasure. One of the two is greater—namely, avidity—and the other is lesser.

Liberality is intermediate between stinginess and wastefulness, and courage is intermediate between rashness and cowardice. Wittiness is intermediate between impudence and wantonness [on the one hand] and dullness [on the other] with respect to jesting, playfulness, and what is related to them. Humility is a moral habit intermediate between pridefulness [on the one hand] and disparagement or familiarity [on the other]. Respectfulness is a moral virtue intermediate between haughtiness, swaggering, or vainglory [on the one hand] and self-abasement [on the other]. Gentleness is intermediate between [37] excessive anger and not becoming angry at anything at all. Modesty is intermediate between insolence and being tongue-tied. Friendliness is intermediate between surliness and flattery. And similarly for the rest of them.

19. Aphorism. What is equilibrated and intermediate is spoken of in two ways. One is what is intermediate in itself and the other what is intermediate in relation and by analogy to another.

What is intermediate in itself is like six being intermediate between ten and two, for the increment of ten over six is like the increment of six over two. This is what is intermediate in itself between two extremes. And every number resembles this in the same way. This intermediate neither increases nor decreases, for what is intermediate between ten and two is at no moment other than six.

What is intermediate in relation does increase and decrease at different times and in accordance with the differing in the things to which it is related. For example, the equilibrated nutriment for a youth and that which is equilibrated for a completely industrious man differs in accordance with the difference in their bodies. What is intermediate for one of the two is other than what is intermediate for the other with respect to extent and number, thickness and softness, heaviness and lightness, and, in general, with respect to quantity and quality. Similarly, an equilibrated climate is in relation to bodies. That condition of being equilibrated and being intermediate with respect to nutriments and medicaments is only increased and decreased in [38] quantity and quality in accordance with the bodies that are being treated, in accordance with their power, in accordance with the art of the sick person,[18] in accordance with the country he is in, in accordance with his previous customs, in accordance with his age, and in accordance with the power of the medicament in itself—so that with respect to a single ailing person the quantity of a single medicament is made to differ in accordance with the difference of the seasons.

This intermediate is the intermediate that is used with respect to actions and with respect to moral habits, for the quantity of actions in number and extent and their quality in intensity and lassitude ought to be determined only in accordance with the relation to the one acting, the one to whom the action is [directed], and that for the sake of which the action is [done]; in accordance with the time; and in accordance with the place. With anger, for example, what is equilibrated with respect to it is in accordance with the condition of the one at whom one is angry, in accordance with the thing for the sake of which there is anger, and in accordance with the time and place in which it occurs. Similarly, the quantitative and qualitative extent of the beating in[19] punishments is in accordance with the one beating and the one beaten, in accordance with the offense for which there is a beating, and in accordance with the instrument by which the beating [is given]. It is similar with respect to the rest of the actions. For what is

18. That is, in accordance with the art or trade the sick person pursues.

19. Reading *fī*, with the Feyzullah manuscript, rather than *wa* ("and"), with Najjar and the other manuscripts.

intermediate in every action is what is determined in relation to the things the action encompasses. The things to which the different actions are compared [39] so as to be determined are not the same in number for every action. Rather, this action is determined in relation to five things, for example, and another action [in relation] to fewer or more than five things.

20. Aphorism. What is intermediate with respect to nutriments and medicaments is what is intermediate and equilibrated for most of the people most of the time; sometimes it is what is equilibrated for one sect apart from another at a certain time and sometimes for a single body at a single time—either long or short. So, too, some of what is intermediate and equilibrated with respect to actions may be what is equilibrated for all of the people or for most of them most or all of the time; some may be what is equilibrated for one sect apart from another at a certain time; and some is what is equilibrated for a single sect at a certain other time while some is what is equilibrated for a single human being at a single time.

21. Aphorism. The one who extrapolates and infers what is intermediate and equilibrated with respect to nutriments and medicaments, however it occurs, is the physician. The art by which he extrapolates that is medicine. The one who infers what is intermediate and equilibrated with respect to moral habits and actions is the governor of cities and the king. The art by which he extrapolates that is the political art and the kingly craft. [40]

[C. HOUSEHOLDS, DWELLINGS, AND CITIES]

22. Aphorism. "City" and "household" do not mean merely the dwelling for the Ancients. But they do mean those whom the dwelling surrounds, whatever the dwellings, of whatever thing they are, and whether they are beneath the earth or above it—being wood, clay, wool and hair, or any of the other things of which the dwellings that surround people are made.

23. Aphorism. Dwellings may engender different morals in their inhabitants. For example, dwellings of hair and leather in the desert engender in their inhabitants the states of character of alertness and resoluteness. Sometimes the matter intensifies to the point that courage and boldness are engendered. Inaccessible and fortified dwellings engender in their inhabitants states of character of cowardice, security, and fright. So it is

obligatory for the governor to keep an eye on the dwellings. Yet that is accidental and only for the sake of the morals of their inhabitants and as a means of assistance.

24. Aphorism. The household is joined together and made prosperous from definite parts and partnerships. They are four: husband and wife, master and slave, father and child, property-holder[20] and property. The one who governs these parts and partnerships, brings some into concert with others, and ties each to the other [41] so that from all of them there is a partnership with respect to actions and a mutual assistance in perfecting a single purpose and in completing the prosperity of the household through good things and preserving them for the members[21] is the lord of the household and its governor. He is called lord of the household and is in the household like the governor of the city is in the city.

25. Aphorism. Both the city and the household have an analogy with the body of the human being. The body is composed of different parts of a definite number, some better and some baser, adjacent to one another in rank, each doing a certain action, so that from all of their actions they come together in mutual assistance to perfect the purpose of the human being's body. In the same way, both the city and the household are composed of different parts of a definite number, some baser and some better, adjacent to one another in a rank of different ranks, each performing on its own a certain action, so that from their actions they come together in mutual assistance to perfect the purpose of the city or the household. Even though the household is a part of a city and households are in the city, their purposes are nonetheless different. Yet there comes together from those different purposes, when they are perfected and brought together, a mutual assistance for perfecting [42] the purpose of the city.

That, too, has an analogy with the body. Indeed, the head, chest, stomach, back, hands, and feet are to the body as the households of the city are to the city. The action of each of the large members is other than the action of the other, yet the parts of each of these large members mutually assist one another in their different actions for perfecting the purpose of that large member. Then, when the different purposes of the large members are

20. Reading *qānin*, for sense, rather than *qunya* ("acquisition").

21. That is, the members of the household; but the text has merely the masculine plural "for them" (*'alaihim*).

mutually perfected, there comes together from them and from their different actions mutual assistance for perfecting the purpose of the whole body. The case of the households with respect to themselves and that of the households with respect to the city is similar. Thus it is that by coming together, all the parts of the city are useful to the city and are useful for constituting some by means of others, as it is with the members of the body.

26. Aphorism. The physician treats each member that is ill only in accordance with its relationship to the whole body and to the members adjacent to it and tied to it. He does so by giving it a treatment that provides it with a health by which it is useful to the whole of the body and is useful to the members adjacent to it and tied to it. In the same way ought the governor of the city to govern every one of the parts of the city, whether it is a small part such as a single human being or a large one like a single household. [43] He treats it and provides it with good in relation to the whole of the city and to each of the rest of the parts of the city by endeavoring to make the good that part provides a good that does not harm the whole of the city or anything among the rest of its parts, but rather a good useful to the city in its entirety and to each of its parts in accordance with its rank of usefulness to the city.

When the physician is not heedful of this, but is intent upon providing one of the members with health and treats it without keeping in mind the condition of the rest of the members adjacent to it, or treats it by means of what harms the rest of the other members, he provides it with a health by which it performs an action that is not useful to the body in its entirety or to the members adjacent to it and tied to it. That makes the member and the members tied to it ill, and its harm is communicated to the rest of the members so that the body in its entirety becomes corrupted. So, too, the city.

When a single member [of the body] is touched by corruption of which it is feared that it will be communicated to the rest of the other members adjacent to it, it is amputated and done away with for the sake of preserving those others. So, too, when a part of the city is touched by corruption of which communication to others is feared, it ought to be ostracized and sent away for the improvement of those remaining. [44]

27. Aphorism. It is not unknown for a human being to have the ability to infer what is intermediate with respect to actions and moral habits as pertains to himself alone, just as it is not unknown for a human being to have

the ability to infer what is intermediate and equilibrated among the nutriments by which he nourishes himself alone. His doing that is a medical action, and he [thereby] has an ability concerning a part of the medical art. Similarly, the one who infers what is equilibrated among moral habits and actions as pertains to himself alone does that only insofar as he has an ability concerning a part of the political art.

However, when the one who has the ability to infer what is equilibrated for one of his members is not heedful that what he infers be without harm for the rest of the parts of the body and does not set it down so as to be useful for the whole [body] and for its parts, his inferring that by means of a part of [the] medical art is corrupt. So, too, if a human being who has the ability to infer what is equilibrated for himself in particular from among the moral habits and actions does not endeavor in what he infers for what is useful to the city or to the rest of its parts, but pays no attention to that or does pay attention to it but does not keep its harmfulness to them in mind, his inferring that by means of a part of [the] political art is corrupt. [45]

28. Aphorism. The city may be necessary and may be virtuous. The necessary city is the one whose parts mutually assist one another in obtaining only what is necessary for a human being's constitution, subsistence, and preservation of life. The virtuous city is the one whose inhabitants mutually assist one another in obtaining the best things for a human being's existence, constitution, subsistence, and preservation of life.

One group is of the opinion that that best is the enjoyment of pleasures, and others are of the opinion that it is wealth. And there is a group of the opinion that the bringing together of both is what is best. Now Socrates, Plato, and Aristotle are of the opinion that human beings have two lives. One is constituted by nutriments and the rest of the external things we require daily for our constitution, and it is the primary life. The other is the one whose constitution is in its essence without having need of external things for constituting its essence. Rather, it is sufficient unto itself for maintaining [its] preservation and is the final life.

For human beings have two perfections, a primary one and a final one. Indeed, the final one is attained for us in this life and in the final life[22]

22. Reading *yuḥṣal lanā fī hādhihī al-ḥayā wa fī al-ḥayā al-akhīra*, with the Diyarbekir, the Chester Beatty, and both of the University of Teheran manuscripts. Najjar, following the other manuscripts, adds *lā* ("not") and *lākin* ("but") so as to read *yuḥṣal lanā lā fī hādhihī al-ḥayā wa lākin fī al-ḥayā al-akhīra* ("is attained for us not in this life but in the final life").

when the primary perfection in this life of ours has preceded it. Primary perfection [46] is that all of the actions of the virtues be done, not that a human being merely possess virtue without doing its actions; and that perfection consists in doing, not in acquiring, the states of character by which the actions come to be. Similarly, the perfection of the scribe is to do the actions of writing, not to acquire writing; and the perfection of the physician is to do the actions of medicine, not merely to acquire medicine. And so, too, with every art.

By means of this perfection the final perfection is attained for us, and that is ultimate happiness, which is the good without qualification. It is what is preferred and yearned after for its own sake and is not—not at any moment at all—preferred for the sake of something else. The rest of what is preferred is preferred only for the sake of its usefulness for obtaining happiness, and each thing becomes good only when it is useful for obtaining happiness. And whatever obstructs from it in some way is an evil.

So the virtuous city according to them is the one whose inhabitants mutually assist one another in obtaining the final perfection, which is ultimate happiness. Therefore it follows that its inhabitants, as distinct from [those of] the rest of the cities, are particularly those possessing virtues. For the city whose inhabitants are intent upon mutually assisting one another to obtain wealth or to enjoy pleasures do not need all of the virtues to obtain their goal. Rather, it might be that they need not even a single virtue. That is because the concord and justice they sometimes use among themselves are not virtue in truth; it is only something resembling justice and is not justice. So, too, with the rest of what they use among themselves in what is analogous to the virtues. [47]

29. Aphorism. In relation to the things they encompass, actions that are equilibrated, intermediate, and determined ought to be useful for obtaining happiness—along with the rest of their stipulations. And the one who extrapolates them ought to set happiness before his eyes, then consider how he ought to determine the actions so that they emerge as useful either to the inhabitants of the city in their entirety or to one or another of them for obtaining happiness. So, too, does the physician set health before his eyes when he is intent upon inferring what is equilibrated with respect to the nutriments and medicaments by which he treats the body.

[D. ON THE KING IN TRUTH]

30. Aphorism. The king in truth is the one whose purpose and intention concerning the art by which he governs cities are to provide himself and the rest of the inhabitants of the city true happiness. This is the goal and the purpose of the kingly craft. It necessarily follows that the king of the virtuous city be the most perfect among the inhabitants of the city in happiness since he is the reason for their being happy.

31. Aphorism. One group is of the opinion that the goal intended in kingship and the governance of cities is majesty; honor; domination; executing command and prohibition; and being obeyed, made great, and magnified. They prefer honor for its own sake, not for any other thing they might gain by means of it. They set down the actions by which cities are governed as actions by which they arrive at this purpose, and they set down the traditional laws of the city as traditional laws by which they arrive at this purpose through the inhabitants of the city. Some arrive at that by practicing virtue [48] with the inhabitants of the city, acting well toward them, bringing them to the good things that are good things according to the inhabitants of the city, preserving these for them, and giving them preference in these things over themselves. They gain great honor thereby, and these are the most virtuous among the rulers of honor. Others are of the opinion that they will become deserving of honor by means of wealth, and they endeavor to be the wealthiest inhabitants of the city and to be themselves unique in wealth so as to achieve honor. Some are of the opinion that they will be honored for descent alone. Others do that by conquering the inhabitants of the city, dominating them, humiliating them, and terrorizing them.

Others among the governors of cities are of the opinion that the purpose of governing cities is wealth. They set down as the actions by which they govern cities actions by which they arrive at wealth. And they set down traditional laws for the inhabitants of the city by means of which they arrive at wealth through the inhabitants of the city. If they prefer a certain good or do anything, they prefer it and do it only so that they attain wealth. It is known that there is a major difference between one who prefers wealth so as to be honored for it and one who prefers honor and to be obeyed so that he will become affluent and arrive at wealth. The latter are called the inhabitants of the vile rulership.

Others among the governors of cities are of the opinion that the goal of governing cities is the enjoyment of pleasures.

A group of others is of the opinion that it is all three of these brought together—namely, honor, wealth, and pleasures. They rule despotically and set [49] the inhabitants of the city down as things similar to tools for them to gain pleasures and wealth.

Not one of these is called king by the Ancients.

32. Aphorism. The king is king by means of the kingly craft, the art of governing cities, and the ability to use the kingly craft at any moment whatsoever as a rulership over a city—whether he is reputed for his art or not, finds the tools to use or not, finds a group who accepts him or not, is obeyed or not. So, too, the physician is a physician by means of the medical craft—whether he is recognized[23] by people for it or not, is furnished with the tools of his art or not, finds a group who serves him by executing his actions or not, comes upon sick persons who accept his statement or not. Nor is his medicine diminished by his not having any of these. Similarly, the king is king by means of the craft and the ability to use the art—whether he has dominion over a group or not, is honored or not, is wealthy or poor.

A group of others is of the opinion that they not apply the name king to anyone who has the kingly craft without [50] being obeyed and honored in a city. Others add wealth to that. And others are of the opinion to add to that dominion by conquest, humiliation, terror, and provoking fear.

None of these is among the stipulations of kingship. Yet they are results[24] that sometimes follow the kingly craft, and it is therefore presumed that they are kingship.

[E. THE INTELLECTUAL VIRTUES]

33. Aphorism. The theoretical rational part and the calculating rational part each has a virtue of its own. The virtue of the theoretical part is the theoretical intellect, knowledge,[25] and wisdom. The virtue of the calculating part is the practical intellect, prudence, discernment, excellent opinion, and correct presumption.

23. The term is *ʿarafa;* see note 5.

24. Literally, "reasons" (*asbāb*).

25. The term is *ʿilm*, which can just as easily be translated as "science." However, here, in aphorisms 34–37, and in aphorism 52, Alfarabi seems to be using *ʿilm* in the sense of "knowledge," and its plural, *ʿulūm*, in the sense of "sciences."

34. Aphorism. The theoretical intellect is the faculty by which we attain, by nature and not by examination or syllogistic reasoning, certain knowledge concerning the necessary, universal premises that are the principles of the sciences. That is like our knowing that the whole is greater than its part, that amounts equal [51] to a single amount are mutually equal, and premises resembling these. These are the ones from which we begin and come to knowledge of the rest of the theoretical beings that are such as to exist without human artifice. This intellect may be potential as long as it has not attained these first [things]. When it attains them, it becomes an intellect in act and of a powerful disposition for inferring what remains. With respect to what it attains, it is not possible that error befall this faculty; indeed, it is not possible for anything pertaining to the sciences to befall it other than what is certainly accurate.

35. Aphorism. The name "knowledge" applies to many things. However, the knowledge that is a virtue of the theoretical part is for the soul to attain certainty about the existence of the beings whose existence and constitution owe nothing at all to human artifice, as well as about what each one is and how it is, from demonstrations composed of accurate, necessary, universal, and primary premises of which the intellect becomes certain and attains knowledge by nature.

This knowledge is of two sorts. One is becoming certain of a thing's existence, the reason for its existence, and of it not being possible for it to be anything else at all—not it nor [52] its reason. The second is becoming certain of its existence and of it not being possible for it to be anything else, but without seizing upon the reason for its existence.

36. Aphorism. Knowledge in truth is what is accurate and certain for all time, not for some [particular time] but not some other, nor existing at one moment and possibly becoming nonexistent afterwards. For if we are cognizant of something existing now and when time passes it is possible for it to be abolished, we are not aware of whether it exists or not. So our certainty comes back as doubt and falsehood, and what can possibly be false is neither knowledge nor certainty.

Therefore, the Ancients did not set down as knowledge the perception of what can possibly change from condition to condition, such as our knowing that this human being is sitting now. For it is possible for him to change and come to be standing after he was sitting. Rather, they set down as knowledge the certainty about the existence of a thing that cannot possibly change, such as three being an odd number. For the oddness of three does not change. That is because three does not become even at some point nor four odd. So if this is called knowledge or certainty, it is done so metaphorically.

37. Aphorism. Wisdom is knowledge of the remote reasons by which all the rest of the beings exist and of the existence of the proximate reasons for the things that have reasons. That is, we become certain [53] of their existence. We know what they are and how they are. And [we know] that even if they are many, they ascend in rank to a single being which is the reason for the existence of those remote things and the proximate things subordinate to them. And [we know] that that single [being] is the first in truth. It is constituted not by the existence of any other thing, but is in its essence so sufficient as not to procure existence from something else. And [we know] that it is not at all possible for it to be a body nor in a body. And [we know] that its existence is another existence, one external from the rest of the beings and not sharing with a single one of them in any meaning at all. Rather, if it shares, it is in name alone and not in the meaning understood from that name. And [we know] that it is not possible for it to be except as one alone. And [we know] that it is the one in truth. It is what provides all the rest of the beings the unity by which we come to say of every existing thing that it is one. And [we know] that it is the true first, the one providing truth to other than it, and is so sufficient in its truth as not to procure truth from something else. And [we know] that it is not possible to fancy a perfection greater than its perfection, much less for it to exist; nor an existence more complete than its existence, a truth larger than its truth, or a unity more complete than its unity.

In addition, we know how the rest of the beings procure existence, truth, and unity from it; what the portion of each one [54] of them is in existence, truth, and unity; how the rest of the things procure thingness from it; and that it makes known[26] the ranks of all the beings—some being first, some intermediary, and some last. The last have reasons that are not reasons for anything subordinate to them. The intermediate are the ones that have a reason over them and are reasons for things subordinate to them. The first is a reason for what is subordinate while having no other reason over it.

26. Reading *wa an yuʿallim*, with the Diyarbekir and Feyzullah manuscripts, rather than *wa an nuʿallim* ("and that we make known"), with Najjar and the Chester Beatty as well as the Bodleian manuscripts.

In addition, we know how the last ascend to the intermediate, how some of the intermediate ascend to others until they end up at the first, and then how governing begins with the first and extends through each one of the rest of the beings in order until it ends up at the last beings.

So this is wisdom in truth. This name is used metaphorically so that those who are very skillful and become perfect in the arts are called the wise.

38. Aphorism. Practical intellect is the faculty by which a human being—through much experience in matters and long observation of sense-perceptible things—attains premises by which he is able to seize upon what he ought to prefer or avoid with respect to each one of the matters we are to do. Some of these premises are universal, and matters we ought to prefer or avoid are enveloped in each one. [55] Some are isolated and particular; they are used as examples for what a human being wants to seize upon of matters he has not observed.

This intellect remains a potential intellect only as long as experience has not been attained. When experiences have been attained and preserved, it becomes an intellect in act. And this intellect that is in act increases along with the increase in experiences with each of the years of a human being's life.

39. Aphorism. Prudence is the ability for excellent deliberation and inference concerning the things that are better and more appropriate for a human being to do to attain a truly major good and a virtuous, venerable goal—whether that be happiness or something of major value for gaining happiness.

Cleverness is the ability for excellent inference concerning what is more virtuous and appropriate for obtaining certain slight goods.

Cunning is the ability for sound deliberation in inferring what is more appropriate and better in order to complete something major [56] with respect to what is presumed to be a good—that is, affluence, pleasure, or honor.

Fraudulence, deception, and deceitfulness concern excellently inferring what is more intense and better for completing some base deed presumed to be a good—that is, base profit or base pleasure.

All of these are things that merely lead to the goal, but are not the goal. So, too, every deliberation. For a human being merely sets the goal for which he has a passion and longing in his calculation; then, afterwards, he deliberates about the things by means of which he may gain that goal—how many they are, what they are, and how they are.

40. Aphorism. Body and soul each have pleasures and pains. The pleasures of each are congruous and suitable things, while the pains are conflicting and adverse things. Pleasures and pains are each either essential or accidental. Essential pleasure is experiencing something congruous, and accidental pleasure is losing a conflicting pain. Essential pain is experiencing what is incompatible, and accidental pain is losing a congruous pleasure.

41. Aphorism. Because of the corruption of their sense-perception and of their imagination, those who have sick bodies imagine what is sweet to be bitter and what is bitter to be sweet. They form a concept of the suitable as being [57] unsuitable and a concept of the unsuitable as being suitable. Similarly, because those who are evil and who possess defects have sick souls, they imagine that evils are good things and that good things are evils.

Now the one who is virtuous in the moral virtues always has a passion and longing only for goals that are good things in truth, and he sets them down as his purpose and intention. The one who is evil always has a passion for goals that are evils in truth. And because of the sickness of his soul, he imagines them to be good things.

It follows therefore that the prudent person is virtuous in the moral virtues and, similarly, the clever person, whereas cunning and fraudulent persons are evil and possess defects. So it comes about that the prudent person verifies the goal by means of the virtue he has and verifies what leads to the goal by means of excellent deliberation.

42. Aphorism. There are many kinds of prudence. Among them is excellent deliberation for governing the affairs of the household—namely, household prudence. And among them is excellent deliberation for the more serious of that by which the city is governed—namely, political prudence. And among them is excellent deliberation with respect to what is better and more appropriate for obtaining an excellent livelihood and in gaining human goods [58] like wealth, majesty, and other things that in addition to being good are valuable for gaining happiness. Among these is what is advisory, namely, the one that infers what a human being does not use for himself but in order to advise someone else about it—either for governing a household, a city, or something else. And among them is

what is adversarial, namely, the ability to infer a virtuous, sound opinion by which to combat the enemy and the opponent in general or by which to repulse him.

It is likely that for everything a human being is preoccupied with, he needs some part of prudence—either a slight or great [amount], in accordance with the matter he is pursuing. If it is great or major, he will need a more powerful and more complete prudence. And if it is minor or slight, a slight [amount of] prudence will be sufficient.

Prudence is what the public calls intellect. And when this faculty is in a human being, he is called intelligent.

43. Aphorism. Correct presumption is that whenever a human being observes a matter, he—by means of his presumption—always lights upon what is so correct that the matter could not possibly be otherwise.

44. Aphorism. Discernment is the ability to light upon the correct judgment with respect to recondite opinions that are disputed [59] and the power to verify it. So it is excellently inferring what is sound in opinions and is, therefore, one of the kinds of prudence.

45. Aphorism. Excellent opinion is for a human being to possess opinion, or to be excellent in opinion, and to be a human being who is virtuous and good in his actions, then for his statements, opinions, and admonitions to have been tested many times and to have been found pertinent and upright. And when the human being uses them, he ends up at praiseworthy outcomes. Therefore, his speech has come to be accepted—that is, because of the accuracy frequently observed with respect to him—so that the virtue or pertinent judgment and advice he is reputed for exempt him from needing a proof or sign for something he says or advises. It is evident that in verifying an opinion and seizing upon what is correct in it, he seizes and verifies only by means of prudence. This, then, is a kind of prudence.

46. Aphorism. There are two roots one who is deliberating uses to infer the thing he is deliberating about. One is the generally accepted things taken from all or most people. [60] The second is the things attained by experience and observation.

47. Aphorism. The simple person is someone who has an unimpaired imaginative grasp of what is generally accepted concerning what is to be

preferred or avoided, except that he has no experience of the practical affairs of which one becomes cognizant through experience. A human being may be simple with respect to one sort of affairs and not simple with respect to another sort.

48. Aphorism. The mad person is one who, with respect to what is to be preferred or avoided, always imagines the contraries of the generally accepted things and the contraries of what is customary. In addition, it sometimes happens that he imagines the contrary of what is generally accepted about the rest of the matters found in much of what is perceived by the senses.

49. Aphorism. Stupidity is when someone's imaginative grasp of generally accepted things is unimpaired and he has preserved experiences. His imaginative grasp of the goals he has a passion and longing for is unimpaired, and he deliberates. But his deliberation inevitably makes him imagine that what does not lead to that [particular] goal does lead to it, [61] or it makes him imagine that what leads to the contrary of that goal leads to it.[27] So his action and advice are in accordance with what his corrupt deliberation makes him imagine. Therefore, when first observed, the stupid person has the form of an intelligent person, and his intention is a sound intention. Frequently, his deliberation lands him in evil, even though he was not aiming to fall into it.

50. Aphorism. Quick-wittedness is excellence in surmising something quickly in no time or in time not delayed.

51. Aphorism. Prudence and cleverness each have need of a natural disposition with which a human being is endowed. When a human being is endowed with a disposition for complete prudence and then becomes accustomed to vices, he is altered and changes. Thus instead of having prudence, he comes to have cunning, deceitfulness, and trickery.

52. Aphorism. A group of people calls the prudent wise. Wisdom is the most excellent knowledge of the most excellent beings. Yet since only human things are perceived by means of prudence, it ought not to be wis-

27. That is, that it leads to the goal in question.

dom unless human beings are the most excellent of what is in the world and the most excellent of the beings. Since human beings are not like that, [62] prudence is wisdom only metaphorically and as a simile.

53. Aphorism. It is particularly characteristic of wisdom that it knows the ultimate reasons for every ultimate being.[28] And the ultimate goal for the sake of which the human being comes about is happiness, the goal being one of the reasons. Therefore, wisdom is what seizes upon the thing that is truly happiness.

Moreover, it is wisdom alone that knows the first one—that from which the rest of the beings procure virtue and perfection. And it knows how that is procured from it and the extent of the portion of perfection each one gains. Now the human being is one of the beings that procure perfection from the first one. Therefore, it knows the greatest perfection that the human being procures from the first—namely, happiness.

Wisdom, therefore, is what seizes upon happiness in truth, whereas prudence is what seizes upon what ought to be done so that happiness is attained. These two, therefore, are the two mutual assistants in perfecting the human being—wisdom being what gives the ultimate goal, and prudence being what gives the means by which that goal is gained.

54. Aphorism. Rhetoric is the ability to speak to others by means of statements that are excellent in persuading about each and every one of the possible matters that are such as to be preferred [63] or avoided. However, the virtuous practitioners of this faculty use it with respect to good things, while those who are cunning use it with respect to evil ones.

55. Aphorism. Excellence in imaginative evocations[29] is other than excellence in persuasion. The difference between the two is that what is

28. See aphorism 37. There, Alfarabi says that wisdom leads us to know "the one in truth . . . and that it makes known the ranks of all the beings—some being first, some intermediary, and some last." The term translated there as "last" is *akhīr*, whereas the term translated here as "ultimate" is *muta'akhkhir*.

29. The term is *takhyīl* and is the verbal noun (*maṣdar*) of *khayyala*. Heretofore Alfarabi has used the verb *khayyala* in conjunction with its reflexive form (*takhayyala*) in contexts that permitted it to be translated as "to imagine" or "to make imagine." Now, however, the sense is that the imagination causes an image to come about in a person's mind, that is, to be evoked.

intended by excellence in persuasion is for the hearer to do something after assenting to it. What is intended by excellence in imaginative evocation is to inspire the soul of the hearer to seek or to flee the thing imaginatively evoked, or to have an inclination to or loathing for it, even if he has not assented to it. This is like a human being feeling disgust when he sees something that resembles what is such as to be truly disgusting, even if he is certain that what he sees is not the thing that is disgusting.

Excellence in imaginative evocation is used with respect to what annoys and contents, with respect to what frightens and assures, with respect to what softens the soul, with respect to what hardens it, and with respect to the rest of the accidents of the soul. What is intended by excellence in imaginative evocation is that a human being be moved [64] to accept something and be inspired toward it, even if what he knows about the thing requires the converse of what is imaginatively evoked. Many people love or detest something, or prefer or avoid it, only due to imaginative evocation, to the exclusion of deliberation, either because they naturally have no deliberation or because they have rejected it in their affairs.

56. Aphorism. All poems are brought forth only to make excellent the imaginative evocation of something, and they are of six sorts. Three are praiseworthy and three blameworthy.

Of the three that are praiseworthy, one is intent upon improving the rational faculty, directing its actions and calculation toward happiness, making an imaginative evocation of divine matters and good things, making an excellent imaginative evocation of the virtues while presenting them favorably and treating them with respect, and presenting evil things and defects as base and vile.

The second is intent upon improving and equilibrating those accidents of the soul related to power and breaking them down until they come to equilibrium and are brought back from the extreme. These are the accidents like anger, self-conceit, harshness, arrogance, impertinence, love of honor, tyranny, avidity, and similar things. And it directs its practitioners to use them [65] for good things to the exclusion of evil ones.

The third is intent upon improving and equilibrating those accidents of the soul related to weakness and softness, namely, the base yearnings and pleasures, delicateness and slackness of soul, compassion, fear, fright, distress, bashfulness, indulgence, softness, and similar things. [It is intent] upon breaking [them down] and bringing them back from the extreme until they come to equilibrium. And it directs to their being used for good things to the exclusion of evil ones.

The three blameworthy ones are the contraries of the three praiseworthy ones. For the former corrupt everything the latter improve and draw it away from being equilibrated to the extreme. The sorts of melodies and songs following from these sorts of poems and their divisions are equivalent to their divisions.

[F. THE VIRTUOUS CITY]

57. Aphorism. There are five parts of the virtuous city: the virtuous, the linguists, the assessors, the warriors, and the moneymakers. The virtuous are the wise, the prudent, and those who have opinions about major matters. Then there are the transmitters of the creed and the linguists; they are the rhetoricians, the eloquent, the poets, the musicians, the scribes, and those who act in the same way as they do and are among their number. The assessors are the accountants, the engineers, the doctors, the astronomers, and those who act in the same way as they do. The warriors are the combatants, the guardians, and those who act in the same way as they do and are counted among them. The moneymakers are those who earn money [66] in the city, like the farmers, herders, merchants, and those who act in the same way as they do.

58. Aphorism. The rulers and governors of this city are of four sorts.

One is the king in truth; he is the supreme ruler and the one in whom six stipulations come together: wisdom, complete prudence, excellent persuasion, excellent imaginative evocation, bodily capability for struggle, and having nothing in his body that prevents him from carrying out the things pertaining to struggle. One in whom all of these qualities come together is the model, someone to be copied in his ways of life and his actions, someone whose declarations and counsels are to be accepted, and one who may govern as he thinks and wishes.

The second is for no human being to exist in whom all of these have come together. But they do exist dispersed among a group so that one of them gives the goal, the second gives what leads to the goal, the third has excellent persuasion and excellent imaginative evocation, and another the capability for struggle. So this group all together takes the place of the king, and they are called superior rulers and the possessors of virtues.[30] Their rulership is called the rulership of the virtuous. [67]

The third is for these not to exist either, so the ruler of the city is then the one in whom [the following] exist together: [a] that he is knowledgeable of the preceding divine and traditional laws[31] the first leaders brought forth to govern cities; [b] then, that he is excellent at distinguishing the places and conditions in which one ought to apply those traditional laws in accordance with the intention of the first [leaders]; [c] then, that he has the capability to infer what was not explicitly declared in the previous traditional laws that were preserved and written down, following in the traces of the prior traditional laws in what he infers; [d] then, that he has excellent opinion and prudence with respect to the events that occur one by one and, not being such as to have come about in the previous ways of life, are such as to preserve the prosperity of the city; [e] that he is excellent in persuasion and imaginative evocation; [f] and that he has, in addition, the capability for struggle. This one is called the traditional king and his rulership is called traditional kingship.

The fourth is for no single human being to exist in whom all of these come together; yet they are dispersed among a group. So altogether they take the place of the traditional king, and these as a group are called traditional rulers.

59. Aphorism. In each of the parts of the city there is a ruler who has none of the inhabitants of that section over him as a ruler, a person ruled who has no rulership over any human being at all, and someone who is a ruler over those beneath him while being ruled by those above him.

60. Aphorism. Some ranks in the virtuous city have priority over others in [different] ways. [68]

[a] Among them is that if a human being has performed a deed in order to obtain a certain goal and has used a certain thing that is the goal of an action another human being carries out, the first is the ruler and has priority over the second in rank. Horsemanship is like that. Its goal is the

30. Reading *al-faḍā'il*, with the Chester Beatty and Feyzullah manuscripts, rather than *al-faḍl* ("surplus" or "superfluity"), with Najjar and the Bodleian as well as the Diyarbekir manuscripts, or *al-faḍīla* ("*virtue*"), with both of the University of Teheran manuscripts.

31. The terms are *al-sharā'i'* (sing. *sharī'a*) and *sunan* (sing. *sunna*).

excellent use of weapons. So the horseman, who uses the reins and the implements of the horse that are the goal of the art of making the reins, is a ruler who has priority over the one who makes the reins and, similarly, over the trainer of the horse. And it is like that in the rest of the accomplishments and arts.

[b] And among them is for there to be two whose goal is one in itself. One of the two is more complete in imaginatively evoking that goal, more perfectly virtuous, possessing prudence by which he infers everything for arriving at that goal, and finely prepared so as to use someone else to attain the goal. This one is a ruler over the second who does not have that.

Subordinate to this one is someone who imagines the goal by himself, but does not have perfect deliberation for carrying out everything by which he gains the goal. Yet if he is given the starting point[32] of deliberation by some of what he wants to do being sketched out for him, he takes what is given [69] as a pattern for what is sketched out and infers what remains.

Subordinate to this one is someone who neither imagines the goal by himself nor has any deliberation. But when he is given the goal, with it being imaginatively evoked for him, and is then given the starting point of deliberation, he is able to take what has been sketched out for him as a pattern for what remains and to do it or to use another for it.

Subordinate to this one is someone who does not imagine the goal, has no deliberation, and is not able—even when given the starting point of deliberation—to infer the remaining. Yet if he is counseled concerning all he ought to do to obtain that goal, he remembers the counsel and is so pusillanimous and submissive as to rush to do all that he is counseled. If he does not know the goal at which that action might culminate, yet is finely prepared to do the thing he is counseled, this one is always a servant of the city and not a ruler; rather, he is a slave by nature.

Now those are the ones who are ruled and who are rulers. Everything the slave and servant are skilled in doing, the ruler ought to be skilled in using someone else to do.

[c] The third [rank] is for there to be two persons, each one of whom performs an action, with a third person using their two actions to complete a certain goal. However, one of the two does something that is more venerable and of greater value for [70] completing the goal of the third. So the one whose action is more venerable and of greater value has priority

32. The term here and in the rest of this aphorism is *mabda'*; in aphorism 34 it was translated as "principle," and in the next aphorism, it is translated as "beginning."

of rank over the one who carries out an action that is viler and of less value with respect to that goal.

61. Aphorism. Some of the parts and ranks of the parts of the city are in concert with others. They are bound by love, and they hold together and stay preserved through justice and the actions of justice. Love may come about by nature, like the love of parents for the child. And it may come about by volition in that its starting point is voluntary things followed by love. That which is by volition is threefold: one is by sharing in virtue; the second is for the sake of what is useful; and the third is for the sake of pleasure. Justice follows upon love.

In this city, love first comes about for the sake of sharing in virtue, and that is connected with sharing in opinions and actions. The opinions they[33] ought to share in are about three things: the beginning, the end, and what is between the two. Agreement of opinion about the beginning is agreement of their opinions about God, may He be exalted, about the spiritual beings, and about the devout who are the standard; how the world and its parts began; how human beings began to come about; then the ranks of the parts of the world, the link of some to others, and their level with respect to God—may He be exalted—and to the spiritual beings; then the level [71] of human beings with respect to God and to the spiritual beings. So this is the beginning. The end is happiness. What is between the two is the actions through which happiness is gained.

When the opinions of the inhabitants of the city are in agreement about these things and that is then perfected by the actions through which happiness is gained for some with others, that is necessarily followed by the love of some for others. Because they are neighbors of one another in one dwelling and some of them need others while some of them are useful to others, that is also followed by the love that comes about for the sake of the useful. Then, due to their sharing in the virtues and because some of them are useful to others, some take pleasure in others. So that is also followed by the love that comes about for the sake of pleasure. So by this they are in concert and bound.

62. Aphorism. Justice first has to do with dividing the shared goods that belong to the inhabitants of the city among them all. Then, after that, [it

33. That is, the citizens, the verb being in the third-person masculine plural (*an yashtarikū*).

has to do] with preserving what has been divided among them. Those goods are security, monies, honor, ranks, and the rest of the goods it is possible for them to share in. Indeed, each one of the inhabitants of the city has a portion of these goods equivalent to what he deserves. His falling short of that or exceeding it is injustice. His falling short is an injustice upon himself, and his exceeding is an injustice upon the inhabitants of the city. And perhaps his falling short is also an injustice upon [72] the inhabitants of the city.

When they [the goods] have been divided and a portion settled upon each one, the portion of each one of those [persons] ought afterward to be preserved. Either it is not to go out of his hand or it is to go out through stipulations and conditions such that no harm touches him or the city from some of his portion going out of his hand. A human being's portion of goods goes out of his hand either by his volition—as with selling, donating, and lending—or not by his volition—as with robbery or usurpation. In each of these two instances, there ought to be stipulations by which the goods of the city remain preserved for the people.[34]

That comes about only by returning, in place of what voluntarily or involuntarily went out of his hand, a good equivalent to that which went out of his hand—either of the [same] kind as what went out of his hand or of another kind. And what is returned is either returned to him personally or to the city. To whichever of the two the equivalent is returned, [73] justice is that the divided goods remain preserved for the inhabitants of the city. And injustice is for someone's portion of the goods to go out of his hand without its equivalent being returned to him or to the inhabitants of the city. Further, what is returned to him personally ought either to be useful to the city or not harmful to it.

When the one causing a portion of the goods to go out of his own hand or out of the hand of another harms the city, he is also unjust and is [to be] prevented. To prevent many, there is need to inflict evils and punishments. The evils and punishments ought to be measured so that for each injustice there is an apposite measured punishment prescribed as an equivalent for it. So, when the evildoer gets a portion of evil, that is justice. When it is excessive, that is an injustice upon him personally; and when it falls short, that is an injustice upon the inhabitants of the city. And perhaps being excessive is an injustice upon the inhabitants of the city.

34. Literally, "for them" (*ʿalaihim*).

63. Aphorism. Some governors of cities are of the opinion that every injustice occurring in the city is an injustice upon the inhabitants of the city. Some of them are of the opinion that it is an injustice particular to that one alone to whom the injustice has occurred. And some of them divide injustice into two sorts. One sort is an injustice particular [74] to individual persons; yet they nonetheless set it down as an injustice upon the inhabitants of the city. And there is a sort they set down as an injustice particular to a single person,[35] but not extending beyond him to the city.

Therefore, a group of governors of cities is not of the opinion that the criminal is to be excused, even if he is excused by the one to whom the injustice has occurred. Some of them are of the opinion that the criminal is to be excused when he is excused by the one to whom the injustice has occurred. And some of them are of the opinion that some are to be excused and some not excused. That is, when the evil a criminal merits is set down as a right particular to the one to whom the injustice has occurred, disregarding the inhabitants of the city, and that human being has excused him, no one else is to have access to him. When that is set down as a right of the inhabitants of the city or of all people, no account is taken of excusing by the one to whom the injustice has occurred.

64. Aphorism. Justice may be spoken of in another, more general, way[36]—namely, a human being practicing acts of virtue, any virtue whatever, with respect to what is between him and someone else. The justice having to do with dividing and the one having to do with preserving what has been divided is a species of the more general justice, and the more particular is called by the name of the more general.

65. Aphorism. Each one in the virtuous city ought to be assigned [75] a single art to which he devotes himself and a single work he undertakes, either in the rank of servitude or in the rank of rulership, but not extending beyond it. For three reasons, not one of them is to be left to pursue many works nor more than a single art. One is that it does not always happen that every human being is suited for every work and for every art; rather, one human being may be found to be suited for one work as distinct from another human being for another work. The second is that

35. Literally, "particular to him" (*yakhuṣṣuh*).
36. Literally, "species" or "kind" (*nawʿ*).

in undertaking a work or an art, every human being does it more perfectly and more virtuously and becomes more skilled and wiser in work when he devotes himself to it, is raised in it from his youth on, and does not busy himself with anything other than it. The third is that for many works there are [particular] times; when they are delayed, they slip away. It may happen that there are two works that are due at a single time. If he busies himself with one of them, the [time for the] other slips away; nor is it caught up with at a subsequent time. Therefore a single human being ought to be devoted to each of the two works so that each of the two works is caught up with at its time and does not slip away. [76]

66. Aphorism. The city's reserve[37] is the monies set aside for the classes who do not usually earn money. According to the opinion of all governors of cities, those who are such and for whom monies are set aside first of all and as a first intention are the divisions of the city whose crafts do not have as primarily intended goals the earning of monies—like the transmitters of the creed, the scribes, the physicians, and their like. For these are among the major parts of the city and have need of monies.

According to the opinion of a group of governors of cities, [they also include] the chronically ill and those who do not have the stamina to earn monies. And a group is of the opinion that no one is to be left in the city who is unable in any way to undertake any of the actions useful to it.

A group of governors of cities is of the opinion that they should set up two reserves of monies in the city: a reserve for those whose crafts do not have as primarily intended goals the earning of monies and a reserve for the chronically ill and those who are in the same situation. So where it ought to be taken from and in what ways must be looked into.

67. Aphorism. War is [a] for repulsing an enemy coming upon the city from outside. Or it is [b] for earning a good the city deserves from outside, from one in whose hand it is. Or it is [c] for carrying and forcing a certain group to what is best and most fortunate for them in themselves, as distinct from others, when they have not been cognizant of it on their own and have not submitted to someone who is cognizant of it [77] and calls them to it by speech. Or it is [d] warring against those who do not submit

37. The term is *'udda* and refers to apparatus or equipment, as well as to what one sets aside as provision against misfortune.

to slavery and servitude, it being best for them and most fortunate that their rank in the world be to serve and to be slaves. Or it is [e] warring against a group not of the inhabitants of the city against whom they have a right, but they withhold it. And this is something shared with two [of the preceding] concerns: [one is] earning a good for the city and the other is that they be carried to give justice and equity.

Now [f] warring against them in order to punish them for a crime they perpetrated—lest they revert to something like it and lest others venture against the city in emulation of them—falls in general under earning a certain good for the inhabitants of the city, bringing that other people back to their own allotments and to what is most proper for them, and repulsing an enemy by force. And [g] warring against them to annihilate them in their entirety and to root them out thoroughly because their survival is a harm for the inhabitants of the city is also earning a good for the inhabitants of the city.

Unjust war is [a] for a ruler to war against a people only to humiliate them, make them submissive, and have them honor him for nothing other than extending his command among them and having them obey him; or [b] only to have them honor him for nothing other than having them honor him; or [c] to rule them and govern their affairs as he sees fit and have them comply with what he knows of what he has a passion for, whatever it is. Similarly, [d] if he wages war in order to tyrannize—not for anything other than setting tyranny down as the goal—then that is also unjust war.

Similarly, [e] if he wages war or kills only to satisfy a fury or for a pleasure he will gain when he triumphs—not for anything other than that—then that is also unjust. Similarly, [f] if those people have made him furious through an injustice and what they deserve because of that injustice is less than warfare and killing, then warfare and killing are unjust without doubt. [78] Many of those who intend to satisfy their fury by killing do not kill those who made them furious, but kill others who have not made them furious. The reason is that they intend to remove the pain that comes from the fury.

[G. THE DIVISIONS OF BEING AND THE STATUS OF HAPPINESS: SOUND VS. ERRONEOUS OPINIONS]

68. Aphorism. The first divisions are three: what cannot possibly not exist, what cannot possibly exist, and what can possibly exist and not

exist. The first two are extremes, and the third is intermediate between them. It is an aggregate that requires the two extremes. All existing things fall under two of these three [divisions]. For some beings cannot possibly not exist, and some can possibly exist and not exist.

69. Aphorism. What cannot possibly not exist is such in its substance and nature. And what can possibly exist and not exist is also such in its substance and nature. For it is not possible that what cannot possibly not exist becomes like that due to its substance and its nature being otherwise and its happening to become like that. So, too, with what can possibly exist and not exist.

There are three genera of existing things: those devoid of matter, celestial bodies, and material bodies.[38] What cannot possibly not exist is of two types: for one, it is in its nature and its substance to exist at a [certain] moment, anything else not being possible for it; the second is what cannot possibly not exist at any time whatsoever. The spiritual are of the second of the sorts that cannot possibly not exist and the celestial of the first, while the material[39] are of the division of what can possibly exist and not exist.

There are three worlds: spiritual, celestial, and material.

70. Aphorism. The first divisions are four: what cannot possibly not exist at all, what cannot possibly exist at all, what cannot possibly not exist at a certain moment, and what can possibly exist [79] and not exist. The existence of what cannot possibly not exist at a certain moment is also possible at a certain[40] moment. So the first two are opposite extremes, whereas it is possible for what can possibly exist not to exist.

71. Aphorism. Existent things are of these three divisions: what cannot possibly not exist at all, what cannot possibly not exist at a certain

38. The term is *al-ajsām al-hayūlāniyya* and thus might be more literally rendered as "bodies of primordial matter"; in the rest of the aphorism, "material" is used to translate *al-hayūlāniyya* or *hayūlāniyya*.

39. In each instance, only the feminine adjective with the definite article is used (*al-rūḥāniyya, al-samāwiyya,* and *al-hayūlāniyya*); the two likely antecedents are bodies (*al-ajsām*) or existing things (*al-mawjūdāt*).

40. Adding *mā*, with the Chester Beatty manuscript.

moment and exist at a certain moment,[41] and what can possibly exist and not exist. The most virtuous, most venerable, and most perfect of them is what cannot possibly not exist at all. The vilest and most defective is what can possibly exist and not exist. That which cannot possibly not exist only at a certain moment is intermediate between the two, for it is more defective than the first and more perfect than the third.

What can possibly exist and not exist is of three types: for the most [part], for the least [part], and equally. The most virtuous of them is that which comes about for the most [part]; the vilest of them is that which comes about for the least [part]; and that which is equal is intermediate between them.

72. Aphorism. That something admits of privation is a defect in its existence. That it needs something else for its existence is also a defect in existence. Whatever has something similar to it in its species is also defective in existence. For that comes about only [a] with respect to what is not sufficient to have its own unique species and [b] with respect to what does not suffice to complete that [species's] existence alone—such that only a portion of that existence comes to be completed by it and it is not sufficient for completing all of it, as with the human being. For since it is not possible to attain human existence by means of a single person, more than one is needed at one time. Thus, whatever is sufficient for completing a certain thing has no need of there being a second with respect to that thing. [80] If something suffices to complete its existence, whatness, and substance, it is not possible for there to be anything else of its species. And if that were with respect to its action, nothing else would share in it[s action].[42]

73. Aphorism. Whatever has a contrary is defective in existence. For whatever has a contrary has privation—this being the meaning of con-

41. For "certain," see the preceding note. Stated in this fashion, and the text appears to be consistent, the clause points to non-existence: "what cannot possibly . . . exist at a certain moment." Though the full statement of the preceding aphorism does admit of such an interpretation, the more immediate sense is that Alfarabi is expressing the idea, albeit obscurely, that "the existence of what cannot possibly not exist at a certain moment is also possible at a certain moment." The phrase also points, again obscurely, to the principle of the excluded middle.

42. Alfarabi seems to be suggesting here that insofar as human beings need to cooperate with one another and to make use of other beings to obtain or acquire the necessities of life, not to mention the virtues, they are not self-sufficient.

traries, namely, that each one of them nullifies the other when they meet or come together. That is because for its existence it depends upon the extinction of its contrary. Moreover, there is an impediment to its existence; thus, it does not suffice simply by itself for its existence. So what does not have privation does not have a contrary, and what has no need at all of anything other than its essence has no contrary.

74. Aphorism. Evil does not exist at all, not in anything of these worlds and, in general, in that whose existence is not at all due to human volition. Rather, all of that is good. That is because evil is of two types. One is the misery opposite to happiness. And the second is everything such that misery is obtained by means of it. Misery is evil in that it is the goal one comes to without there being beyond that a greater evil to which one comes by means of misery. The second is the voluntary actions such as to lead to misery.

Similarly, opposite to these two evils are two goods. One is happiness, and it is a good in that it is the goal without there being any other goal beyond it sought by means of happiness. The second good is everything useful in any way for obtaining happiness. So this is the good opposite to it. And this is the nature of each one of the two, nor does evil have any nature other than the one we have mentioned.

So both evils are voluntary and, similarly, the two goods opposite to them. The good in the worlds is the first reason, everything following from it, what follows from what follows from it, and that whose existence follows from what follows from it, [81] on to the ultimate consequences.[43] And, according to this ranking, any evil that is.[44] So all these are according to order and justice based on desert, and anything reached through desert and justice is good.

43. Or, in keeping with the translation of *lazama* thus far in this clause as "to follow," "on to the ultimate things that follow" (*ilā ākhir al-lawāzim*).

44. Reading *ayy sharr kāna*, with Najjar and all of the manuscripts except the Chester Beatty, which reads *ayy shai' kāna* ("anything that is"). The different readings point to a major problem of interpretation: though the aphorism opens with Alfarabi denying that evil has any existence at all, this particular argument starts from the premise that all good—even that in the worlds—is contrary to all evil and that both are merely voluntary. That leaves room for evil being discussed here as a consequence of the first reason or first cause, as reflected in the majority of the manuscripts. Note, however, the final sentence of this aphorism.

In speaking throughout this aphorism of "worlds" (*'awālim*), rather than of "two worlds" (*'ālamān*)—that is, what is evoked as God's dominion in the opening lines of the Quran—Alfarabi indirectly calls that description into question.

A group presumed that existence, whatever it might be, is good and that non-existence, whatever it might be, is evil. So on their own they fashioned chimeric beings that they set down as good and non-existent beings that they set down as evil.

Others presumed that pleasures, whatever they might be, are goods and that pain, whatever it might be, is evil—especially the pain attaching to the sense of touch.

All of these are in error. That is because existence is good only when it is deserved, and non-existence is evil when it is not deserved. So, too, pleasures and pain. Existence and non-existence that are not deserved are evil, and none of these is something existing in anything of the spiritual worlds. For no one presumes that anything that is not deserved takes place in the spiritual and the celestial [worlds]. Nor does anything that is not deserved take place in the natural possible [worlds], as long as what is deserved is upheld in them; nor is what is voluntarily deserved sought in them. In possible nature, what is deserved is either in form or in matter. What each thing deserves is either for the most [part], for the least [part], or equally. Everything it gains that does not go beyond these is therefore good.

So there are two types of good.[45] One type has no evil opposite to it at all, and one type does. Similarly, every natural thing whose principle is a voluntary action may be a good and may be an evil. Now the discussion here concerning what is purely natural shares in no way with the voluntary. [82]

75. Aphorism. A group presumes that all the accidents of the soul and what comes from the appetitive part of the soul are evils. Others are of the opinion that the faculties of yearning and anger are both evil. And others are of that opinion concerning the other faculties by which the passions of the soul come about, like jealousy, harshness, greed, love of honor, and what is similar.

These are also in error. That is because it is not what is suitable for being used for both good and evil that is good or evil, for one of the two is not more likely [to occur] than the other. So they are either both good and evil, or neither the one nor the other is. Rather, each one of these is evil

45. Reading *fa-al-khair idhan ḍarbān*, with the Chester Beatty manuscript, rather than *fa-al-khairāt ḍurūb* ("so there are types of good things"), with Najjar and the other manuscripts.

when it is used to gain misery. Whereas when they are used to gain happiness, they are not evils; rather, all of them are goods.

76. Aphorism. One group says that happiness is neither a reward for [performing] the actions by which happiness is gained, nor a recompense for giving up the actions by which it is not gained. For the knowledge attained through learning is not a reward for the learning that preceded it, nor a recompense for the rest that would have occurred had he not been learning and thus given it up, preferring toil in its stead. Moreover, if the knowledge gained from learning were followed by pleasure, that pleasure would not be a requital for instruction nor a recompense for the concomitant toil and pain when he preferred instruction, and gave up rest, so that this pleasure might be a recompense for another pleasure he gave up in order to be recompensed for it by this other one. Rather, happiness is a goal such that it is gained by virtuous actions in the same way as knowledge is attained by learning and study, and as the arts are attained through learning them and persisting in their activities. Nor is misery punishment for giving up virtuous actions or a requital for doing defective ones. [83]

Therefore anyone who believes this about happiness and is, in addition, of the opinion that what he is recompensed by,[46] for what he gives up, is of the genus of what he gives up has virtues that are close to being defects. That is, the moderate person who gives up all or some sensual pleasures only so as to be compensated in place of what he gave up with another pleasure of a genus greater than what he gave up is carried by his avidity and covetousness for augmenting pleasure to give up what he gives up. Moreover, it must be his opinion that what he gave up was his; he gave it up only to come to something like it and to an increase in profit. Otherwise, how would he be recompensed for giving up what is not his?

The case is the same with justice. For the justice that is practiced by giving up money and not taking it is also only avidity and covetousness for what he is to gain and be compensated for by his giving it up. He gives it up only out of covetousness for profit and to be recompensed for what he gives up with something far greater than what he gives up. It is as though he is of the opinion that all monies are his, what belongs to him

46. Reading *yuʿawwaḍ*, for sense, with Dunlop, rather than *yafūtuh* ("he relinquishes") with Najjar and all of the manuscripts.

and what belongs to everybody. But he leaves it for them when he is able and capable of usurping it from them so that several times more will come to him from the source.

That is like what the usurer does. He does not acquire justice and moderation insofar as they are a good for their own sake, nor does he give up doing evil and defective things for its own sake or because it is base in itself.

The case is the same with the courageous person among these. He is of the opinion that he relinquishes the pleasures he wants for this fleeting life so as to be compensated for that by pleasures of a kind far greater than what he relinquished. He advances boldly upon an evil he loathes from fear of a greater evil. For he is of the opinion that advancing boldly upon death is an evil, yet fears an evil greater than it.

Therefore, these that are presumed [84] to be virtues are closer to being vices and vile things than to being virtues. That is because their substance and nature are not truly of the nature of virtues nor close to it, but are rather of the genus of defects and vile things.

77. Aphorism. By death, the virtuous person only relinquishes doing more of what increases happiness after death. Therefore, his apprehensiveness about death is not the apprehensiveness of someone who is of the opinion that by death he will gain a very major evil nor the apprehensiveness of someone who is of the opinion that by death he will relinquish a major good he has already attained and that will go out of his hand. Rather he is of the opinion that he will not gain any evil at all by death. He is of the opinion that the good he has attained at the time of his death is with him and will not separate from him at death. Rather, his apprehensiveness is only the apprehensiveness of someone who is of the opinion that he relinquishes a profit he would have gained had he remained, one increasing what he had attained of good. It is close to the apprehensiveness of someone who is of the opinion that what he relinquishes is not capital but a gain he was estimating and hoping for. So he is not at all frightened, but loves surviving so as to increase the good activity by which happiness is increased.

78. Aphorism. The virtuous person ought not to hasten death, but ought rather to employ stratagems to survive as long as it is possible to increase doing what makes him happy lest the inhabitants of the city lose the usefulness of his virtue to them. He ought to advance boldly upon death only when there is greater usefulness to the inhabitants of the city by his dying

than by his surviving. When death reluctantly alights upon him, he ought not to be apprehensive but virtuous. He should not be at all apprehensive about it nor be so frightened of it as to become distracted. Only the inhabitants of ignorant and immoral cities are apprehensive about death.

For [the inhabitants of] the ignorant [cities], it is because of their relinquishing the goods of this world that they leave behind by death—these being either pleasures, monies, [85] honors, or ignorant goods other than that. For the immoral person, it is because of two things. One is his relinquishing what he leaves behind of this world. The second is because he is of the opinion that he relinquishes happiness by death. With respect to that, he is more apprehensive than [the inhabitants of] the ignorant [cities]. For the inhabitants of the ignorant [cities] know nothing of happiness after death so as to be of the opinion that they relinquish it. The former do know of it and so at death, due to what they presume they are relinquishing, apprehension and sorrow attach to them along with great repentance for what they have embarked upon previously in their lives. Thus they die while being distressed in several ways.

79. Aphorism. When the virtuous warrior puts himself at risk, he does not do so while judging that he will not die through that action of his; for that is stupidity. Nor does he not let come to mind whether he will die or live, for that is rashness. Rather, he is of the opinion that he will perhaps not die and will perhaps escape. But he is not frightened by death, nor does he become apprehensive when it lights upon him.

He does not put himself at risk while knowing or presuming that he will gain what he seeks without risk. Rather, he puts himself at risk only when he knows that what he seeks will be relinquished and not gained if he does not take the risk. He is of the opinion that he will perhaps gain it if he takes the risk. Or he is of the opinion that the inhabitants of the city will without doubt gain it through that action of his, whether he dies or lives. And he is of the opinion that if he is unharmed, he will share [it] with them; and that if he dies, they will gain it[47] while he will achieve happiness because of his previous virtue and because he has now sacrificed himself.

80. Aphorism. When the virtuous person dies or is killed, he ought not to be mourned. Rather the inhabitants of the city ought to be mourned

47. Reading *nālūh,* with the Chester Beatty manuscript, rather than *nāl* ("he will gain"), with Najjar and the other manuscripts.

according to the extent of his value to it, and he is to be admired in keeping with the extent of his happiness in the condition he has come to. And the warrior killed in warfare is singled out to be praised for sacrificing himself on behalf of the inhabitants of the city and for his boldness before death. [86]

81. Aphorism. A group of people are of the opinion that the human being who is not wise becomes wise only by the separation of the soul from the body, in that the body remains without having a soul—and that is death. If he were wise before that, his wisdom would thereby be increased, completed, and perfected, or would become more perfect and more virtuous. Therefore, they are of the opinion that death is a perfection and that the soul's being united with the body is a constraint.[48]

Others are of the opinion that the evil human being is evil due only to the soul's being united with the body and that he becomes good with its being separated. Thus, it is incumbent upon these [people] to kill themselves and to kill others. They subsequently have recourse to saying: "We are governed by God, by the angels, and by the helpers of God; of ourselves, we do not control the body's being united with the soul, nor its being separated from it; so we ought to wait for the One who united them to loose [them] and not help in their loosing ourselves. That is because those who govern us are more knowledgeable about what improves us than we are."

Others are of the opinion that the separation of the soul from the body is not a separation in place nor a separation in idea, nor is the body destroyed while the soul survives or the soul destroyed while the body survives without possessing a soul. Rather, the meaning of the soul's being separated is that for its constitution it does not need the body to be its matter, nor in anything pertaining to its actions does it need to use a tool that is a body or use a faculty in a body. Nor in anything pertaining to its actions does it at all need to have recourse to an action of a faculty in a body. For as long as it is in need of one of these things, it is not separated.

That pertains only to the soul particularly characteristic of the human being, namely, the theoretical intellect. For when it comes to this state, it becomes separated from the body regardless of whether that body is liv-

48. Reading *qasr*, with the Chester Beatty manuscript, rather than *fa-sharr* ("evil"), with Najjar and the Bodleian, Feyzullah, and both of the University of Teheran manuscripts, or *qishr* ("covering"), with the Diyarbekir manuscript.

ing in that it is nourished and is sense perceptive, or whether the faculty by which it is nourished and is sense perceptive [87] has already been abolished. For if with respect to anything pertaining to its actions it comes not to need sense perception or imagination, it will already have come to the afterlife. Then its[49] forming a concept of the essence of the first principle will be more perfect, since the intellect will have seized its essence without needing to form a concept of it by means of a relationship or an example. It does not arrive at this state except by its previous need for having recourse to the bodily faculties and their actions for performing its [own] actions.[50] This is the afterlife in which a human being sees his Lord, not being defrauded in his seeing nor disquieted.

82. Aphorism. Anything whose existence comes about by means of combination and composition, however that combination and composition come about, is defective in existence because of its constitution's needing the things of which it is combined—whether that is a combination of quantity, a combination of matter and form, or any other of the sorts of combinations.

83. Aphorism. That one thing acts upon another is for that other to follow from the thing, and one thing acting upon another is that other following from the thing. One thing is an agent of another when it [the latter] follows from it. The agent of something is what makes that thing follow from it. That by which the other is acted upon[51] is that from which the other cannot possibly follow as long as it is not moved. That is, whenever it has procured by its movement a state by which alone it acts or a state added to what it had previously, it acts upon that other by the coming together of the second and the first; so by those two having come together, it acts upon [88] that other. That pertains only to what was existing at first with an insufficiency to act until another thing was added to it. What has acted upon another only by being moved is in its substance needy and insufficient to make follow another thing such as to follow from it to generate what is such as to be generated and to act upon what is such as to be acted upon. Therefore, whatever is sufficient in its substance and in its

49. The antecedent of the masculine singular pronoun can only be the theoretical intellect (*al-ʿaql al-naẓarī*), as is borne out by the sequel.

50. Reading *afʿālah*, for sense, rather than *afʿālahā* ("their actions").

51. Reading *yufʿal al-ākhar bih*, with the Chester Beatty manuscript, rather than *yufʿal ākhar fīh*, with Najjar and the other manuscripts.

own existence to act upon another does not at all act upon what it acts upon nor make follow what it makes follow by being moved.

84. Aphorism. Anyone who does a certain thing knows that his doing that thing at a certain moment is more beneficial or is good, or [that his] doing that thing is not more beneficial or is evil. He postpones doing that only because there is an impediment to his doing that thing. The corruption he is of the opinion and knows will occur to that thing if he does it at that moment is what impedes him. So he ought to know what the reason for corruption is at that moment and what the reason for improvement is afterward. If there is no reason for corruption, then it is not more appropriate that it not be than that it be. So why should it not come about? Moreover, does its artisan have the ability to extinguish the corruption occurring when it is done at that moment or not? If he does have the ability, its occurring[52] is not more appropriate than its not occurring, nor is its coming to be at any moment impossible for its artisan.

If he does not have the ability to extinguish the corruption, the cause[53] of the corruption is more powerful. So of himself the artisan is not completely sufficient for that thing's coming to be without qualification. In addition, there is something contrary to his action and impeding it. At any rate, he is therefore not sufficient by himself for completing that action; rather, it is he, plus[54] the extinction of the reason for corruption and the presence of the reason for improvement. For if he in and of his own essence were the reason for improvement, the improvement coming from the action ought not to have been postponed[55] in time, but they should both come to be simultaneously. Therefore it follows that when the agent [89] in and by himself suffices for generating a certain thing, the existence of that thing is not postponed after the existence of the agent.

85. Aphorism. It is said that a human being is intelligent and that he intellects when two things have come together in him. One is that he be excellent at distinguishing what actions he ought to prefer or avoid. The second is that he practice what is most excellent with respect to everything he seizes upon by means of his excellence at distinguishing. For

52. That is, the occurrence of the corruption.
53. Literally, "reason"; the term is *sabab*.
54. Adding *wa*, with the Diyarbekir manuscript.
55. Reading *muta'akhkhar*, with the Chester Beatty manuscript, rather than *muzāyad* ("extended"), with Najjar and the other manuscripts.

when he is excellent at distinguishing and practices what is worse and more vicious with respect to what he distinguishes, it is said that he is a propagandist, a fraud, or a deceitful person.

Our saying that "so and so has intelligence now" may be used in place of our saying "he has become aware of what he was neglecting" and may be used instead of our saying "he has understood what the expression of the speaker signified" and "it has been impressed upon his soul." We may say "he has intellected," meaning thereby that the intelligibles have reached him as concepts and impressions in his soul. And we say of him "he is intelligent," meaning by our statement "the intelligibles have reached his soul"; that is, that he knows the intelligibles. For there is no difference here between saying "he intellects" and saying "he knows," between "the one who is intelligent" and "the one who knows," or between "things intellected" and "things known."

According to the opinion of Aristotle, the prudent person is one who has excellent deliberation for inferring what virtuous actions he ought to do at a certain moment with respect to each occurrence if, in addition, he is virtuous with respect to moral virtue. What the dialecticians mean by saying that "this is affirmed by intelligence or refuted by intelligence" is what is generally accepted by everyone according to unexamined opinion. For they call intelligence the unexamined opinion shared by everyone or by most people.

86. Aphorism. A group of people say of the first cause[56] that it does not intellect or know [anything] other than its essence.

Others claim that it attains all of the universal intelligibles in one fell swoop and that it knows them and intellects them simultaneously in no time. For they all come together in its essence, [90] always known to it in actuality forever and ever.

Others claim that despite attaining the intelligibles, it knows all of the sense-perceptible particulars and forms a concept of them, and that they are impressed upon it. And [they claim] that it forms a concept of and knows what is now non-existent but will exist hereafter, what has been in the past and is bygone, and what exists now. It is incumbent upon these [people] that accuracy, falsehood, and mutually contrary beliefs succeed one another in all of the intelligibles it has; that those intelligibles be unending; that those of them that are affirmative become negative as well

56. Literally, "reason"; the term is *sabab*. See note 53.

as that those that are negative become affirmative at another time; and that it know unending things with respect to what is past. That is, that it knows what will be in the future and that it knows what is existing now. And, moreover, that it knows what had been, then was existing for times without end before that instant, namely, the conjectured moment; and afterward it knows those known things for times without end in ways different from what it knows of those very things at another moment.

If I set down an example of that, it will become evident and apparent to you. So let the example be set down as the time of Hermes or of Alexander. What it knew in the time of Alexander as coming to be in the present time, which is close to the moment of that time, it[57] had known for many stretches of time before that it would be; and it knows afterward, in another time, that it has been. So it knows that thing to be existing in the time that was in Alexander's time according to three times and three conditions of knowledge. That is because, before the time of Alexander, it knows that it will be; in the time of Alexander himself, it knows that it is presently in being; and afterward, it knows that it has been, then became exhausted, and expired.

It is like that if you compare the condition of each time or the condition of each year, month, or day in spite of the frequency of numbers and the difference of conditions. [91] It is the same with the condition of individuals and the sorts of changeableness succeeding upon one individual after another. For example, it knows that Zayd is a helper of God, obedient and useful to His helpers; then it knows him as an enemy of God, disobedient and harmful to His helpers. So, too, with the conditions of land, the movements of spatial bodies, and the transformation of some into others. Now this opinion eventually brings its proponents to repulsive, base things. From it, wicked opinions branch off that are the reason for major evils in addition to its baseness, the types of changeableness and transformations that become incumbent upon the soul of the knower, the incidents succeeding upon them, and what is similar to that.

87. Aphorism. Many creatures hold different beliefs about God's, may He be exalted, providence for His creatures.

Some claim that He provides for His creatures just as the king provides for his flock and their welfare—without becoming directly involved in each one of their affairs, nor acting as a mediator between his associate

57. Reading *qad*, with the Chester Beatty manuscript, rather than *wa qad* ("and it had"), with Najjar and the other manuscripts.

and his wife. Rather he sets in place for that someone who takes it over, carries it out, and does with respect to it what truth and justice oblige him to do.

Others are of the opinion that that is not enough unless He takes over for them and takes upon Himself, on their behalf, the governing of each one of His creatures with respect to each thing pertaining to their actions and welfare and does not put any one of His creatures in charge of another. Otherwise, those would be His partners and aides in His governance of His creatures, and He is too exalted to have partners and aides. From that, it follows that He is responsible for[58] many of the actions that are defects, blameworthy things, base things, the error of those who err, and obscene speech and deed. And when any one of His creatures is intent upon tricking one of His helpers or refuting by means of objection the statement of someone who is telling the truth, He would be his aide and the One responsible for directing and guiding him. He would drive this person to fornication, murder, theft, and what is baser than that such as the actions of children, drunkards, and mad persons. Now if they deny some of His governing or aiding, they must deny [92] all of it.

These are the roots of wicked opinions and the reason for corrupt, bad doctrines.

[H. THE VIRTUOUS REGIME]

88. Aphorism. The regime [taken] without qualification is not a genus for the rest of the sorts of regimes, but is rather a kind of ambiguous name for many things that are consistent with it while differing in their essences and natures. There is no partnership between the virtuous regime and the rest of the sorts of ignorant regimes.

89. Aphorism. The virtuous regime is the one through which the leader[59] gains a kind of virtue he cannot possibly gain otherwise, namely, the greatest[60] of the virtues a human being is able to gain. The ruled[61] gain

58. Here and further on in the aphorism the literal sense is "He is the one who takes over" (*huwa al-mutawallī li*).

59. The term is *sā'is* and thus belongs to the same root as *siyāsa*, translated here and throughout the text as "regime."

60. Reading *akbar*, with the Chester Beatty manuscript, rather than *akthar* ("most" or "the most"), with Najjar and the other manuscripts.

61. Or, more literally, "the led" (*al-masūsīn*). This, too (see note 59), belongs to the same root as *siyāsa* ("regime").

virtues with respect to their this-worldly life and the afterlife that they could not gain except by means of it. With respect to their this-worldly life, it is [a] that the body of each one have the best traits possible for its nature to receive, [b] that the soul of each one have the best conditions possible for its individual nature and for its power to [obtain] the virtues that are the reason for happiness in the afterlife, and [c] that their subsistence be better and more pleasant than all the sorts of life and subsistence that others have.

90. Aphorism. It is difficult and improbable that a pure sort of the ignorant regimes not sullied by anything else would follow from the actions of one of the ignorant rulers. For the actions of each one of them stem from his opinion, presumptions, and the exigencies of his soul, not from knowledge or an acquired art. Therefore, what exists are regimes that are a blending of these ignorant regimes or of most of them.

91. Aphorism. The predecessors only regulated these ignorant regimes, because knowledge is preserved and retained only by universal regulations.[62] Yet the existing ignorant regimes [93] are often combined regimes, so that someone cognizant of the nature of each regime is able to recognize what the existing regime is combined from and to pass judgment on it on the basis of what he finds of its combination and on the basis of the nature of every one of the simple sorts [of regimes] he is cognizant of.

The case is the same with all practical things, such as rhetoric, sophistry, dialectic, and the poetic art. For the one who uses them without having any knowledge of them, while only presuming and reckoning that he is using demonstration, is often found to be using a various and sunday mixture of them.

92. Aphorism. Indeed, every one of the sorts of ignorant regimes comprises sorts that are very different and varied. Some are at the limit of badness, and some are slightly harmful while being greatly useful with respect to particular members of a certain group. That is because the condition of regimes and their link to souls is like the condition of the seasons

62. The term is *qawānīn* (sing. *qānūn*), and the verb translated as "regulated" is *qannana*. The substantive refers to law and legislation in the sense of regulation, ordinance, or rule.

and their link to bodies possessing different temperaments. Just as some bodies are improved in temperament and condition in the fall and some improved in the summer, while some find the winter season to be most beneficial and most agreeable for them, and some are greatly improved in the spring, such is the condition of souls ard their link to the regimes.

However, the roots from which bodies are combined are likely to be more strongly restricted than are traits and ways of life. That is because traits and ways of life are combined from natural and voluntary things that are likely to be unending, some intentionally and others fortuitously. Many of the people of the traditional laws[63] mill around in misery without knowing it. Yet that is hardly hidden to the sick and to those possessing bad temperaments, or to the one investigating their conditions.

93. Aphorism. The sorts of experiential faculty differ according to the different places in which it is used, the arts united with it, and those who use it, just as the art of writing differs [94] according to the arts in which it is used and those who use it. That is, what is used of both sorts[64] for governing virtuous cities is very virtuous. Now the prudent person uses the experiential faculty during his youth, in his conduct in the presence of the supreme ruler, and while he is being schooled in virtuous rulership. From it a very venerable faculty useful in the virtuous regime is generated. Eventually, it succeeds in bringing the rulership of the one in whom virtuous rulership is potential to become actual rulership. And the most venerable of the sorts of writing is that used in the service of the supreme ruler and the virtuous king. Yet with respect to the venerable and the virtuous, it is subordinate to the experiential faculty used by the supreme ruler. For what is unqualifiedly venerable with respect to the experiential faculty is more venerable than what is venerable with respect to the art of writing.

What is used of the experiential faculty in the lowest of the ignorant regimes—namely, the tyrannical regime—is evil and more vile than all of it used in the rest of the places. Similarly, what is used of writing in the tyrannical regime is evil and more vile than the sorts of writing used in the rest of the regimes and arts, and than what the rabble uses of it. Just as what is used of writing in the service of the virtuous king and the virtuous

63. Reading *al-sunan*, with Najjar and all of the manuscripts except the Chester Beatty, which has *al-siyar* ("ways of life").

64. As the rest of the aphorism suggests, the two sorts are the experiential faculty and the art of writing.

rulership is more venerable than the rest of the remaining sorts of writing used in the city, so is what is used of writing in the service of tyranny, its harmfulness, and the increase of its evil and tribulation more vile than the rest of the sorts of writing.[65] And just as what the prudent person and the supreme ruler use of the experiential faculty [in ruling] is more venerable than what they use of it in the service of writing, so is what the one devoted to tyranny uses of the experiential faculty [in ruling] more vile than what he uses of it in the service of writing.

In sum, everything venerable surpasses what is subordinate to it in its species [95] when it is used in virtuous rulership; and it is vile and harmful, exceeding in vileness and harmfulness the rest of what is in its species, when it is used in the tyrannical regime. Similarly, the rest of the faculties of the soul that make a human being venerable, like distinguishing and what follows it, are the reason for every good in outstanding people; so they are very venerable and virtuous things. In the evil human being, they are the reason for every evil and corruption. And in the tyrannical king, they are the reason for the multiple evils that come about for one who is not a ruler.

Therefore, they[66] did not call the faculty of calculation by which what is more useful for an evil goal is inferred a virtue of calculation. They called it, rather, by other names—like deceitfulness, ruse,[67] and trickery. Those human things that are the greatest voluntary things and arts in the tyrannical city are likely to be evils, disasters, and reasons for disasters being generated in the world. Due to that, the virtuous person is forbid-

65. The text for this and the preceding sentence is corrupt, perhaps due to an inadvertently omitted clause. Dunlop relies upon a medieval Hebrew translation (Bodleian, Mich. 370) to read the following bracketed clause: *wa ka-dhālika mā yustaʿmal min al-kitāba . . . wa al-ṣināʿāt wa mā yastaʿmiluh al-sūqa ashraf min mā [yustaʿmal min al-kitāba fī khidmat al-taghallub ka-mā an yakūn sharf mā] yustaʿmal min al-kitāba fī khidmat al-malik al-fāḍil . . . aṣnāf al-kitāba*. The *ashraf min ma* ("more venerable than what") just before the bracketed clause is from the Chester Beatty, the only Arabic manuscript to which Dunlop had access for this part of the text; the manuscripts known to Najjar give *wa bi-ḥasab sharf mā* ("and in keeping with the venerableness of what"). If Dunlop's reading along with his emendation were accepted and a *wāw* ("and") were placed before *ka-mā* ("just as") the text would read: "Similarly, what is used of writing . . . and arts. And what the rabble uses of it is more venerable than what is used of writing in the service of tyranny. And just as what is used of writing in the service of the virtuous king . . . the sorts of writing."

For my translation, I follow Najjar and the other manuscripts, except that with the Chester Beatty manuscript I omit the *wāw* preceding the second *ka-dhālika* ("similarly"); see 94: 15.

66. The antecedent is not specified, but the pronoun probably refers to the Ancients.

67. Reading *jarbaza*, for sense, rather than *jarīza* ("outrage").

den to reside in the corrupt regimes, and it is obligatory for him to emigrate to the virtuous cities if any exist in actuality in his time. If they are non-existent, then the virtuous person is a stranger in this world and miserable[68] in life; death is better for him than living.

94. Aphorism. ON THE USES OF THE THEORETICAL PART IN PHILOSOPHY, AND THAT IT IS NECESSARY FOR THE PRACTICAL PART IN [DIFFERENT] WAYS.

One of them is that practice is virtuous and correct only when a human being has (a) become truly cognizant of the virtues that are truly virtues, (b) become truly cognizant of the virtues that are presumed to be virtues yet are not like that, (c) habituated [96] himself to the actions of the virtues that are truly virtues so that they become one of his traits, (d) become cognizant of the ranks of the beings and what they deserve, (e) set each of them down in its level, (f) given it the full share of its right—namely, the extent of what it was given—and of its rank among the ranks of being, (g) preferred what ought to be preferred, (h) avoided what ought to be avoided, and (i) not preferred what is presumed to be preferable nor avoided what is presumed ought to be avoided. This is a state that is not attained or perfected except after becoming sophisticated; perfecting cognizance by means of demonstration; and becoming perfect in the natural sciences, what follows upon them, and what is after them according to rank and order, so that he finally comes to knowledge of the happiness that is truly happiness—namely, that which is sought for its own sake and at no period of time is sought for anything else—and is cognizant of how the theoretical virtues and the virtues of calculation are a reason and principle for bringing about the practical virtues and the arts. This does not come to be as a whole except through pursuing theory and transferring from degree to degree and level to level.

It is not possible in any other way. That is,[69] the one who wishes to learn theoretical philosophy begins with numbers, then ascends to magnitudes, then to the rest of the things to which numbers and quantities pertain essentially—like optics and moving magnitudes—then to the celestial bodies and music, to weights, and to mechanics. These are things that are understood and conceived of without matter. And he ascends little by little in the things that need matter to be understood and conceived of until he comes to the celestial bodies.

68. Literally, "bad" (*radī'*).
69. Adding *wa-dhālika* with the Chester Beatty manuscript.

Then, afterward, it is necessary for him to introduce principles other than the principles of "what," "by what," and "how" to aid him in using the things that it is difficult or impossible to come to intellect unless they come into matter. They are adjacent to, [97] or midway between, the genus that has no principles of existence other than the principles of its [own] existence and the genus for whose species the four principles exist.[70] The natural principles emerge for him, and he pursues them and makes a theoretical inquiry into the natural beings and their principles of instruction until he comes to the principles of existence. What he procures of the principles of existence comes to be a ladder and principles of instruction for him. So the principles of existence he has procured come to be principles of instruction only in relation to two things.[71]

Then he transfers to knowledge of the reasons for the existence of natural bodies and the search for their essences, substances, and reasons. When he ends up at the celestial bodies, the rational soul, and the active intellect, he transfers again to another rank. So it is necessary for him to inquire theoretically into the principles of their existence until he becomes aware of principles that are not natural. Thus, what he has procured of the principles of existence of that third rank also comes to be principles of instruction for these beings that are of more perfect existence than the natural ones.

He also comes to a midpoint between two sciences—the science of natural things and the science of what is after the natural things—in the ranking of investigation and instruction. He also becomes aware of the principles for the sake of which they were brought into being, as well as of the goal and perfection for the sake of which the human being was brought into being. He knows [a] that the natural principles that are in the human being and in the world are insufficient for the human being to come by them to the perfection he was brought into being to obtain and [b] that the human being needs intellectual principles by which he strives toward that perfection.

The human being has already come close to obtaining the level and degree of theoretical knowledge by which he gains happiness. And he obtains theory from both directions until he ends up at a being that can-

70. That is, in addition to the three principles identified in the first sentence of this paragraph, the principle of end—"for what."

71. The two things in question seem to be the two genera: namely, the genus having no principles of existence other than those for its own existence, and the genus that has the four principles of existence.

not possibly [98] have any of these principles at all. Rather, it is the first being and the first principle for all the beings mentioned previously; in ways no defect intrudes upon, but rather in the most perfect of the ways by which something is a principle for the beings, it is the one by which, from which, and for which they exist. He thus attains cognizance of the ultimate reasons for the beings. This is divine theoretical inquiry into the beings. In addition, he is always investigating the purpose for the sake of which the human being was brought into being—namely, the perfection incumbent upon the human being to obtain—and all the things by which the human being obtains that perfection. Then he is able to transfer to the practical part, and it is possible for him to begin to practice what he ought to practice.

Another way is for someone to be given the practical part by a revelation that directs him toward a determination of each thing that he ought to prefer or avoid. They are both called knowers, for the name "knowledge" is homonymous for both of them just as it is homonymous for the practitioner of natural science and the diviner who relates what comes to be with respect to possible things. That is, the diviner does not have the ability to know all the individual possible things, because they are unending; and it is absurd that knowledge would encompass what is unending. Yet he has the ability to set down knowledge of some possible thing that happens to occur to his mind or to the mind of one asking him about it. Because knowledge of some possible thing is knowledge contrary to the nature of the possible, the diviner does not have knowledge about the nature of the possible. Rather, knowledge about the nature of the possible belongs to the practitioner of natural science.

Therefore the knowledge of both of them does not come from one substance but the two are, rather, mutually contrary. The case is similar for someone who has become perfect in theoretical science and someone who has had revealed to him how to determine the actions of the inhabitants of cities or of a city without having cognizance of anything pertaining to theoretical science. Nor is there a link or true congruence between one who has received revelation and who is perfect in theoretical knowledge, and one who has received revelation without [99] having become perfect in theoretical knowledge. Rather, the congruence is in name alone.

95. Aphorism. The virtue of calculation is what enables a human being to make an excellent inference about what is more useful with respect to a virtuous goal shared by nations, a nation, or a city when there is a shared

occurrence. Some of it is inference for what changes over short periods, and this is called the faculty for the sorts of temporary, particular governorships for the occurrence of things that occur gradually to nations, a nation, or a city. The faculty of calculation that infers what is useful for a goal that is evil is not a virtue of calculation.

96. Aphorism. With respect to our bodies, it is not possible for us to acquire all the sorts of health with its temperaments,[72] or its constitutional elements, its customs, the kind of dwelling particular to it, the art by which to make a living, or what is similar to that. This is the condition of most bodies. And in some places, it is possible for the inhabitants to acquire only a slight amount of the sorts of health. The case is the same with [our] souls, in that they cannot acquire the virtues, or most of them, or can acquire only a slight amount of them.

It is not up to the virtuous leader and the supreme ruler to establish virtues in someone the nature and substance of whose soul do not accept the virtues. For souls like this, it is up to him to obtain as much of the virtues as is possible for them and for their existence in accordance with what is useful for the inhabitants of the city. Likewise, for bodies in the condition that has been described, it is not up to the virtuous physician [100] to obtain the most perfect levels nor the highest degrees of health. It is up to him to obtain as much health as is possible for their nature and substance in accordance with the actions of the soul. Now the body is for the sake of the soul, and the soul is for the sake of final perfection—namely, happiness. And with respect to virtue, the soul is for the sake of wisdom and virtue.

[I. THE DOUBTFUL APHORISMS][73]

97. Aphorism. By Abū Naṣr, found appended to the back of the book in the handwriting of al-Khaṭṭābī.[74]

He said: It is not likely to find a human being endowed so perfectly

72. Reading *bi-amzijatihā*, with the Chester Beatty manuscript, rather than *wa amzijatihā* ("and its temperaments"), with Najjar and the other manuscripts.

73. Aphorisms 97–100 are found only in the Chester Beatty manuscript and seem to be the addition of someone else; see Dunlop, p. 95.

74. The identity of this person is not known. Dunlop notes, however (p. 95), that a certain Ḥamd or Aḥmad ibn Muḥammad ibn Ibrāhīm al-Khaṭṭābī, the author of *Ghārib al-Ḥadīth: al-Bayān fī Iʿjāz al-Qur'ān* (The marvelous character of Hadīth: An explanation of the inimitableness of the Quran), was "a younger contemporary" of Alfarabi.

from the outset that no disparity is found in him at all and that the rest of his actions, his way of life, and his moral habits flow according to justice and equity without inclining to any of the extremes or to the tyranny of some contraries over others. That is because the endowed temperament is fabricated from mutual contraries that the composition forces together; if its natural characteristics were left alone and equalized, no compositeness would result from them at all due to the great dissimilarity between them and the disparate variation comprised within them. In spite of their coming together forcibly, there is no security against a slight or major discord bringing about the cessation of equilibrium in the natural constitution. Every endowed temperament having less discord among its elements is closer to equilibrium. And whenever discord becomes greater, it goes further away from equilibrium. Thus the natural constitution flows along with measures of discordance and equilibrium equal to the discordance and equilibrium of its natures.

98. Aphorism. From the discourse of Abū Naṣr, may God be pleased with him.

Set down two men, one of whom already knows what is in all of Aristotle's books pertaining to physics, logic, metaphysics,[75] politics, and mathematics, and all or the bulk of whose actions[76] are in conflict with what is noble according to the unexamined opinion shared by everyone. All of the actions of the other are in agreement with what is noble according to the unexamined opinion shared by everyone, even though he is not knowledgeable about the sciences the first one knows. Now this second one is closer to being a philosopher than the first, all of whose actions are in conflict with what is noble according to the unexamined opinion shared by everyone. And he is more able to master what the first has already mastered than the first to master what the second has already mastered.

Philosophy in truth, according to unexamined opinion,[77] is for a human being to attain the theoretical sciences and to have all of his actions be in agreement with what is noble according to shared unexamined opinion and in truth. The one who is limited to the theoretical sciences

75. Or, alternatively, "divine things" (*al-ilāhiyya*).

76. Reading *af'āluh*, with the Chester Beatty manuscript, rather than *af'āluhā* ("their actions").

77. Reading *fī badī' al-ra'y fī al-ḥaqīqa*, with Najjar, rather than Dunlop's *fī badī' al-ra'y wa fī al-ḥaqīqa* ("in unexamined opinion and in truth").

without all of his actions being in agreement with what is noble according to shared unexamined opinion is hindered by his established customs [101] from doing the actions that are noble according to the unexamined opinion shared by everyone. Therefore it is more likely that his customs will hinder him from having his actions be in agreement with what is noble in truth. And the one whose customary actions[78] are in agreement with what is noble according to the unexamined opinion shared by everyone is not hindered by his customs from learning the theoretical sciences, nor from having his actions come to be in agreement with what is noble in truth. For unexamined opinion compels him to do what is truly obligatory to do[79] more than to do what is an unconsidered opinion according to unexamined opinion. What is truly an opinion is an opinion that has been considered, and verified after consideration. And unexamined opinion makes it obligatory that a considered opinion be sounder than unexamined opinion.

99. Aphorism. Also from the discourse of Abū Naṣr, may God's compassion be upon him.

Association for virtue is beset by no variance at all and no enmity, because the purpose with respect to virtue is one—namely, the good willed for itself, not for anything else. Since what the two[80] yearn for and are intent upon is that purpose which is the good in itself, their path to it is one and their love for the thing itself is one. As long as their purpose is one, there is no enmity between the two of them.

Enmity occurs only through difference in yearnings and variance in purposes. Then the conduct that comes about is one not admitting association. For the purpose of each is not the purpose of the other, nor is the path of one the path of the other. Moreover, in spite of their being analogous, they are corrupt and are an evil, not a good like the first purpose and the first association in seeking truth, obtaining happiness, and loving knowledge and virtuous things.

78. Literally, "whose actions to which he has become accustomed" (*afʿāluh allatī qad iʿtādahā*).

79. Reading an *yafʿal mā huwa fī al-ḥaqīqa wājib fiʿluh*, for sense, rather than an *yafʿal fī al-ḥaqīqa mā huwa wājib fiʿluh* ("to do in truth what it is obligatory to do"), with Najjar and the Chester Beatty manuscript, or an *yafʿal mā huwa fī al-ḥaqīqa jamīl wa wājib fiʿluh* ("to do what is noble in truth and obligatory to do"), with Dunlop.

80. There is no antecedent to which "the two" might refer. As becomes evident in the sequel, at issue are two individuals in each type of regime whose conduct brings about variance and enmity when they do not associate for the sake of virtue.

A second association is an association for earning and mutual support with respect to commercial dealings and business trades, because each one of the traders and partners wants to deny his companion his lot so as to get more. And his companion also wants that from him and believes in it; so then there is variance.

The first two associate for nothing external to themselves and nothing for which they need another; nor is there contact with anyone else. Thus no variance at all comes between them as long as their purpose is one, just as no association at all comes about with these other two as long as their purpose is at variance.

Moreover, the purpose intended in everything is truth and, likewise, good and virtue. So the two seekers of truth have already agreed upon their pursuit; they know it and thus do not disagree about it. What is other than truth and virtue is a path that is not to be traveled. When a human being travels it, he errs and becomes perplexed. The [other] two did not grasp their purpose and were at variance because of the difference in their purpose and because they traveled a path other than the one leading to their pursuit, even though they did not know it. For the pursuit of truth is in the soul by nature, even if it falls short of it. Do you not see that if you were to give each one of them the virtue of truth and knowledge, he would affirm it and know it even if he did not put it to use because of his defect and the accidents attaching to him? [102]

100. Aphorism. What the careless person and the one who feigns carelessness attain is the same. For carelessness leads the careless person to corruption, and feigning carelessness leads the one who feigns carelessness to corruption. So the two of them agree about what is attained, namely, corruption. The one who feigns carelessness is not benefited by being cognizant of what he feigns carelessness about when he has not practiced what is obligatory with respect to it. Nor is the careless person [more] harmed by being absentminded and not doing what is obligatory. For the two of them agree about what is added and vary from one another with respect to knowledge and ignorance.

Enumeration of the Sciences

The translation

This translation is based on the text of the Enumeration of the Sciences edited by ʿUthmān Amīn over half a century ago.[1] More recently, Muhsin Mahdi has corrected Amīn's edition of Chapter Five up through the first two paragraphs of the fifth section.[2] Both the emendations and the numbering of the sections introduced by Mahdi have been adopted here, but I have introduced my own paragraph divisions. The numbers within square brackets in the text refer to the page numbers of Amīn's original edition and are also to be found in the margins of Mahdi's text. The present translation differs from Fauzi Najjar's ear-

1. See *Iḥṣā' al-ʿUlūm li-al-Fārābī*, edited, with an introduction and notes, by ʿUthmān Amīn (Cairo: Dār al-Fikr al-ʿArabī, 1949).

2. See *"Fī al-ʿIlm al-Madanī wa ʿIlm al-Fiqh wa ʿIlm al-Kalām min al-Faṣl al-Khāmis min Kitāb Iḥṣā' al-ʿUlūm"* ("About Political Science, the Science of Jurisprudence, and the Science of Theology from the fifth chapter of the book, *Enumeration of the Sciences*") in *Abū Naṣr al-Fārābī, Kitāb al-Milla wa Nuṣūṣ Ukhrā* (Abū Naṣr al-Fārābī, Book of Religion and other texts), ed. Muhsin S. Mahdi (Beirut: Dar al-Mashriq, 1968), pp. 67–76. In his introduction, Mahdi explains that in revising Amīn's text, he drew upon Angel González Palencia's second edition of *Iḥṣā' al-ʿUlūm—Catálogo de las ciencias*, edited, with Spanish translation (Madrid: Consejo Superior de Investigaciones Científicas, 1953)—as well as the use Palencia made of the Madrid Escurial Library manuscript, no. 646, plus the following manuscripts: Princeton University Library, Yahuda, no. 308; Istanbul Köprülü Library, Mehmet, no. 1604; and Egyptian National Library, Maktabāt, no. 264. The Princeton manuscript is the original from which the photocopy used by Amīn was taken, but neither he nor Palencia knew of the Köprülü manuscript; see Mahdi, pp. 22–27, esp. 26–27.

lier version[3] insofar as it is more literal and thus, hopefully, more faithful to Alfarabi's own prose style.

The argument of the work

In the preface or introduction to the Enumeration of the Sciences, Alfarabi explains that he is intent upon enumerating each of "the well-known sciences" and groups them into five chapters: the science of language and its parts; the science of logic and its parts; the sciences of mathematics, by which he means arithmetic, geometry, optics, astronomy, music, measuring, and engineering; physical science and its parts as well as divine science and its parts; and, finally, political science and its parts, plus the sciences of jurisprudence and dialectical theology. In addition, he points to five ways in which his presentation of these sciences will be useful. They fall under three different headings. First, the book will be useful to the student of a given science for learning what to begin with, what to look into, what is worth looking into, and what is to be gained from studying that science so as to proceed in an orderly manner; similarly, it will allow one to compare the sciences and to learn which are more excellent, more useful, more sure, and more powerful as distinguished from those that are less so. Second, it will be useful insofar as it enables one to discern whether a person claiming to have insight into one of these sciences does in fact have such insight and will permit one who has a good grasp of one of the sciences to discern whether he knows all of its parts or only some, as well as to determine the extent of his knowledge. Finally, it will be useful both to the educated person intent upon gaining a summary acquaintance with each science and to the one who would like to resemble scientific people and thus be thought to be one of them.

The presentation of each science is, accordingly, succinct—even somewhat elementary. But, as is ever the case with Alfarabi, even his most general and unexceptional statements have deeper significance. This is especially true of his account of political science and of the way he contrasts it to jurisprudence on the one hand and dialectical theology on the other.

3. See "*Alfarabi,* The Enumeration of the Sciences," trans. Fauzi M. Najjar, in *Medieval Political Philosophy: A Sourcebook,* ed. Ralph Lerner and Muhsin Mahdi (New York: The Free Press of Glencoe, 1963), pp. 24–30.

Alfarabi devotes roughly the same amount of space to his account of political science as he does to that of the science of dialectical theology, but says surprisingly little about the science of jurisprudence. Moreover, he displays a remarkable ambivalence about what to call these different pursuits: though he always speaks of political science—sometimes contrasting it with, or assimilating it to, political philosophy—he seems unsure whether jurisprudence and dialectical theology are sciences or arts. To be sure, each is identified as a science in the preface to this work as well as in the title to the chapter, and Alfarabi once refers to jurisprudence as a science; but he also speaks of it and of dialectical theology as arts. There is something else: succinct as is Alfarabi's account of jurisprudence, and negative as is his account of dialectical theology, especially his description of the sophistry to which some groups of dialectical theologians resort in order to defend religion, it is only with respect to these two arts or sciences that the term "opinions" occurs. As presented here, the well-known political science or political philosophy concentrates on influencing the way human beings act to such an extent that neither one has anything to say about what they think.

Another striking feature about Alfarabi's short disquisition on political science is its repetitiveness. Indeed, he seems to give two nearly identical accounts of political science in the first and third sections of Chapter Five. But since nearly identical is not the same thing as identical, one must wonder about the difference or differences between these two accounts. Or, if the account of political science and political philosophy presented in the first and second sections represents one statement, and that presented in section three another, the question centers on the differences between the explanation of sections one and two and that of section three. That the first may be a non-philosophic political science is suggested by the fact that the term "political philosophy" appears only in section two and that if Plato and Aristotle are mentioned at all, it is only in section three.[4] If this first political science is not philosophical or based on philosophical reflections, on what is it based?

An equally important question concerns the relationship between Alfarabi's full account of political science (that given in sections 1–3) and both jurisprudence and dialectical theology. The account of these latter two, but especially of dialectical theology, is based on the way they are

4. See *Enumeration of the Sciences*, Chapter 5, section three and note 5.

actually practiced, whereas the account of political science and political philosophy appears to be based more on what each strives for or aims at. That is, neither political science nor political philosophy is presented as though this is the way people think either one actually functions—except when negative examples are adduced. And, as noted, when Alfarabi begins to discuss jurisprudence and dialectical theology, he observes that each is concerned with opinions and actions, a distinction he does not make when speaking about political science or political philosophy. It almost seems as though jurisprudence and dialectical theology are unique in being able to offer people a complete view of the whole, something the old political science or political philosophy cannot achieve. Alfarabi does not attempt here to defend the old political science or political philosophy. Nor does he seek to show that either one can provide an equivalent to the worldview set forth by jurisprudence and dialectical theology. What he does, instead, is to note that jurisprudence and dialectical theology come into being with religion (*milla*), something he is completely silent about in his account of political science and political philosophy.

Still, Alfarabi does indicate how limited dialectical theology is. He does so obliquely, to be sure, but he does it. A regime ruled by adherents to jurisprudence (*fiqh*) and dialectical theology (*kalām*) is not desirable. Rather, it is limiting, even threatening, with respect to independent inquiry. Consequently, we must wonder how Alfarabi can provide for a political science that is capable of competing with the appeal of jurisprudence and dialectical theology and yet keeps open the possibility of inquiry. Given the limitations of this work, we cannot expect to find the solution here; it is to be found in the *Book of Religion*. Indeed, at the end of that work (section 27), Alfarabi explains how the account of political science and religion offered there achieves both of these goals and then concludes by insisting upon the importance of religion for sound political life. A sign that Alfarabi saw the two works linked in this manner is the number of overlapping passages or parallels in the two works: section 1 of the *Enumeration of the Sciences* with sections 11–13, 14, and 14a-d of the *Book of Religion*; section 2 of the *Enumeration of the Sciences* with section 15 of the *Book of Religion*; and section 3 of the *Enumeration of the Sciences* with part of section 15 plus sections 16–18 of the *Book of Religion*. In other words, in the *Enumeration of the Sciences* and above all in Chapter Five of that work, Alfarabi is intent on far more than providing a conventional summary of the sciences or simply preserving for posterity a record of knowledge as it was received at his time. Rather, he seeks to show here the problems that political science and political philosophy have to face now that revealed religion has appeared. An indication of how they can meet that challenge occurs only in the *Book of Religion*.

Enumeration of the Sciences

[102] CHAPTER FIVE:
ON POLITICAL SCIENCE,
THE SCIENCE OF JURISPRUDENCE,
AND THE SCIENCE OF DIALECTICAL THEOLOGY

1. Political science investigates the sorts of voluntary actions and ways of life; the dispositions, moral habits, inclinations, and states of character from which those actions and ways of life come about; the goals for the sake of which they are performed; how they ought to exist in a human being; how to order them in him according to the manner they ought to exist in him; and the way to preserve them for him.

It distinguishes among the goals for the sake of which the actions are performed and the ways of life practiced.

It explains that some of them are truly happiness and that some are presumed to be happiness without being so and that it is not possible for the one which is truly happiness to come to be in this life, but rather in a life after this one, which is the next life, whereas what is presumed to be happiness—like affluence, honor, and pleasures—is what is set down as goals only for this life.

It distinguishes the actions and the ways of life.

It explains that the ones through which what is truly happiness is obtained are the goods, the noble actions, and the virtues; that the rest are evils, base things, and imperfections; and that the way they are to exist in a human being is for the virtuous actions and ways of life [103] to be distributed in cities and nations in an orderly manner and to be practiced in common.

It explains that those do not come about except by means of a rulership that establishes those actions, ways of life, states of character, dispositions, and moral habits in cities and nations and strives to preserve them for the citizens[1] so that they do not pass away; that this rulership does not come about except by a craft and a disposition that bring about the actions for establishing them among the citizens[2] and the actions for preserving for them what has been established among them. This is the kingly craft, or kingship, or whatever a human being wants to call it; and the regime is the work of this craft.[3] And [it explains] that rulership is of two kinds: [a] A rulership that establishes the voluntary actions, ways of life, and dispositions such that by them one obtains what is truly happiness; it is virtuous rulership, and the cities and nations subject to this rulership are the virtuous cities and nations. [b] And a rulership that establishes in cities and nations the actions and states of character by which one obtains what is presumed to be happiness without being such, namely, ignorant rulership. This rulership admits of several divisions, each one of which is called by the purpose it is intent upon and pursues; thus there are as many of them as there are things this rulership seeks as goals and purposes. If it seeks to acquire wealth, it is called a vile rulership; if honor, it is called timocracy; and if something other than these two, it is called by the name of that goal it has.

It explains that the virtuous kingly craft is composed of two faculties. One of these is the faculty for [104] universal rules. The other is the faculty a human being acquires through lengthy involvement in civic deeds, carrying out actions with respect to individuals and persons in particular cities, and skill in them through experience and long observation, as it is with medicine. Indeed, a physician becomes a perfect healer only by means of two faculties. One is the faculty for the universals and the rules he acquires from medical books. The other is the faculty he attains by lengthy involvement in practicing medicine on the sick and by skill in it from long experience with, and observation of, individual bodies. By

1. Literally, "for them" (*ʿalaihim*).

2. Literally, "among them" (*fīhim*).

3. Or, alternatively, "and politics is the activity of this craft" (*wa al-siyāsa hiya fiʿl hādhihī al-mihna*). The difficulty in understanding the precise meaning of the clause arises because the term *siyāsa* can just as well mean "politics" as "regime."

means of this faculty the physician is able to determine the medicaments and cure with respect to each body in each circumstance. Similarly, the kingly craft is able to determine the actions with respect to each occurrence, each circumstance, and each city in each moment only by means of this faculty, which is experience.

2. Political philosophy is limited—in what it investigates of the voluntary actions, ways of life, and dispositions, and in the rest of what it investigates—to universal rules. It gives patterns for determining them with respect to each circumstance and each moment; how, by what, and to what extent they are to be determined. Then it leaves them undetermined, because determining in actuality belongs to a faculty other than this science and is such as to be added to it. Moreover, the circumstances and occurrences with respect to which determination takes place are indefinite and without limitation.

3. This science has two parts.

One part comprises bringing about cognizance of[4] what happiness is; distinguishing between what it truly is and what it is presumed to be; enumerating the universal voluntary actions, ways of life, moral habits, and states of character that are such as to be distributed in cities and nations; and distinguishing the virtuous ones from the non-virtuous ones.

Another part comprises the way of ordering the virtuous states of character and ways of life in the cities and nations; bringing about cognizance of the royal actions by which the virtuous ways of life and actions are established [105] and ordered among the inhabitants of the cities and of the actions by which what has been ordered and established among them is preserved.

Then it enumerates the non-virtuous sorts of kingly crafts, how many they are and what each one is. It enumerates the actions each one of them performs and what ways of life and dispositions each one of them seeks to establish in the cities and nations so as to obtain its purpose from the inhabitants of the cities and nations under its rulership.[5] It explains that

4. See *Selected Aphorisms*, note 5. Here and in what follows, the terms derive from the second form of *ʿarafa* so that at issue is making the citizens aware of, or acquainting them with, something, rather than providing them with knowledge or science about it.

all of those actions, ways of life, and dispositions are like sicknesses for the virtuous cities. The actions that particularly characterize these kingly crafts and their ways of life are like sicknesses for the virtuous kingly craft. The ways of life and dispositions that particularly characterize their cities are like sicknesses for the virtuous cities.

Then it enumerates how many reasons and tendencies there are because of which the virtuous rulerships and the ways of life of virtuous cities are in danger of being transformed into ignorant ways of life and dispositions. Along with them, it enumerates the sorts of actions by which virtuous cities and rulerships are restrained lest they become corrupted and transformed into non-virtuous ones. It also enumerates ways of ordering, tricks, and things to be used to restore them to what they were when they have been transformed into ignorant ones.

Then it explains the number of things that constitute the virtuous kingly craft; [106] among them are the theoretical and practical sciences, and added to them is the faculty attained through experience arising from long involvement in actions with respect to cities and nations, namely, the aptitude for excellently inferring the stipulations by which the actions, ways of life, and dispositions are determined with respect to each community, each city, or each nation in accordance with each circumstance and each occurrence. It explains that the virtuous city remains virtuous and is not transformed only when its kings succeed one another through time and have the very same qualifications[6] so that the successor has the same attributes and qualifications as his predecessor and their succession is without interruption or break. It brings about cognizance of what ought to be done so that there is no interruption in the succession of kings. It explains which natural qualifications and attributes ought to be sought in the sons of the kings and in others

5. In Angel González Palencia's editions of this work, based on the Madrid Escurial manuscript, the following variant is to be found: "And this is in the Politics, namely, the book by Aristotle on politics; and it is also in the Republic by Plato and in books by Plato and others." The clause "the *Republic* by Plato" might also be translated as "the book by Plato on politics," it being almost identical to the clause "the book by Aristotle on politics," that is, *kitāb al-siyāsa li-Aflāṭūn* and *kitāb al-siyāsa li-Arisṭūṭālīs*. The variant is bracketed by both Mahdi and Amīn. Though Amīn had access only to the first edition of Palencia's work—namely, *Catálogo de las ciencias*, edited, with Spanish translation, by Angel González Palencia (Madrid: Maestre, 1932)—Mahdi was able to consult as well the 1953 second edition in which this phrase is also found.

6. Here and in what follows in the rest of this section, the term is *sharā'iṭ* and thus should be understood literally as "stipulations."

so that the one in whom they are found will qualify for kingship after the one who is now king. It explains how the one in whom these natural qualifications are found is to be raised and in what way he ought to be instructed so that he attains the kingly craft and becomes a complete king.

It explains, moreover, that those whose rulership is ignorant ought not to be called kings at all and that they have no need of either theoretical or practical philosophy in any of their circumstances, activities, or ways of ordering; rather, each one of them can achieve his purpose with respect to the city or nation under his rulership by means of the experiential faculty he attains by pursuing the kind of actions with which he obtains what he is intent upon and arrives at the good that is his purpose, [107] providing he happens to possess a deceitful faculty and genius good for inferring the actions he needs for obtaining the good he is intent upon—pleasure, honor, or whatever—and to that is added his being good at imitating those kings who preceded him and were intent upon the same thing as he.

4. The art of jurisprudence is that by which a human being is able to infer, from the things the lawgiver declared specifically and determinately, the determination of each of the things he did not specifically declare. And he is able to aspire to a verification of that on the basis of the purpose of the lawgiver in the religion he legislated with respect to the nation for which it was legislated.

Every religion has opinions and actions. The opinions are like the opinions that are legislated with respect to God, how He is to be described, the world, and other things. The actions are like the actions by which God is praised and the actions by which there are mutual dealings in cities. Therefore the science of jurisprudence has two parts: a part with respect to opinions and a part with respect to actions.

5. The art of dialectical theology is a disposition by which a human being is able to defend the specific opinions and actions [108] that the founder of the religion declared and to refute by arguments whatever opposes it. This art is also divided into two parts: a part with respect to opinions and a part with respect to actions.

It is different from jurisprudence in that the jurist takes the opinions and actions declared by the founder of the religion as given and sets them down as fundamentals from which he infers the things that necessarily follow from them, whereas the dialectical theologian defends the things the jurist uses as fundamentals without inferring other things from them. If it happens that there is a certain human being who has the ability to do both matters, he is a jurist and a dialectical theologian. He defends them insofar as he is a dialectical theologian, and he infers them insofar as he is a jurist.[7]

As for the ways and opinions by which religions are to be defended, [a] one group of dialectical theologians is of the opinion they should defend religions by saying that the opinions of religions and all that is posited in them are not such as to be examined by opinions, deliberation, or human intellects. For they are of a higher order insofar as they are taken from divine revelation and because there are divine secrets in them that human intellects are too weak to perceive and do not reach. Moreover, a human being is such that by revelation religions provide him with what he is not wont [109] to perceive by his intellect and what his intellect is too languid [to grasp]. Otherwise, were revelation to provide a human being only with what he knew and could perceive by his intellect if he considered it, there would be no sense to, or benefit from, it. If it were thus, people would trust in their intellects and they would have no need for prophecy or revelation. But that is not what is done with them. Therefore, with respect to the sciences, religions ought to provide what our intellects are not able to perceive. Not only this, but also what our intellects object to; for whatever we more strongly object to is more likely to be of greater benefit. That is because what religions bring forth that intellects object to and fancies find repugnant is not objectionable or absurd in truth, but is valid according to the divine intellects.

If a human being were to reach the end of perfection with respect to humanity, his position with respect to those who have divine intellects would be that of a child, an adolescent, and an immature youth with respect to a perfect human being. Many children and immature youths object to many things by their intellects that are not objectionable or impossible in truth, although to them they happen to be impossible. And that is like the position of the one at the end of the perfection of the human intellect with respect to the divine intellects. Before being educated and trained, a human being objects to many things, [110] finds them repugnant, and imagines that they are impossible. When he is educated by

7. This marks the end of the Arabic text edited by Muhsin Mahdi. For what follows, the translation is based on ʿUthmān Amīn's edition.

means of the sciences and given training in experiments, those presumptions disappear: the things that were impossible for him are transformed and become necessary, and he now comes to wonder about the opposite of what he formerly used to wonder about. Similarly, it is not impossible that the human being who is perfect in humanity may object to[8] things and imagine they are not possible without them being like that in truth.

So for these reasons,[9] these [dialectical theologians] were of the opinion that religions are to be set down as valid. Indeed, he who brought us revelation from God, may He be exalted, is truthful; it is not permissible that he ever have lied. That he is like this can be validated in one of two ways: either by the miracles he performs[10] or that appear through his hands, or by the testimonies of those truthful ones who preceded him whose statements about his truthfulness and his standing with respect to God, may He be exalted and magnified, are accepted, or by both together. Once we validate his truthfulness and that it is not permissible for him ever to have lied in these ways, there ought to remain no room for intellecting, consideration, deliberation, or reflection with respect to what he says. So by these and similar [ways], these [dialectical theologians] were of the opinion that they would defend religions.

[b] Another group is of the opinion that they defend religion by first setting forth everything stated explicitly by the founder of the religion in the very utterances he expressed. Then they pursue the sense-perceptible, generally received, and intelligible things. When they find one of these things or their consequences, [111] however remote, testifying to what is in the religion, they defend it by means of that thing. When they find one contradicting[11] anything in the religion, and they are able to interpret—even by a very remote interpretation—the utterance by which the founder of the religion expressed it in a way agreeing with that contradiction, they interpret it so. If that is not possible for them, yet it is possible to treat the contradiction as spurious or construe it so as to agree with what is in the religion, they do so. If the testimony of the generally received things is opposed to that of the sense-perceptible things, as when the sense-

8. Reading *lā yamtani' an yastankir*, with the Madrid Escurial manuscript, instead of Amīn's *lā yamtani' min an yakūn yastankir* ("it is not impossible . . . would have objected").

9. Reading *al-asbāb*, for sense, instead of *al-ashyā'* ("things"), with Amīn and the other manuscripts.

10. Reading *ya'maluhā*, with the Madrid Escurial manuscript, instead of *ya'qiluhā* ("that he intellects"), with the text.

11. Correcting *mutāqiḍan* in the text, which has no meaning, to *munāqiḍan*.

perceptible things or their consequences require one thing and the generally accepted things or their consequences require its opposite, they look to the one that has the most powerful testimony for what is in the religion and take it while rejecting the other and treating it as spurious. If it is not possible to construe the utterance in the religion so as to agree with one of these, nor to construe one of these so as to agree with the religion, and it is not possible to reject or treat as spurious any of the sense perceptible, generally received, or intellected things that are opposed to anything in it, they are then of the opinion that the thing may be defended by it being said to be true because it was reported by one for whom it is impermissible to have ever lied or erred. And these [dialectical theologians] say about this part of the religion what those first ones said about all of it. So these [dialectical theologians] are of the opinion that they defend religions in this way.

[112] A group of these [dialectical theologians][12] are of the opinion that they may defend things like this—that is, ones imagined to be repulsive—by pursuing the rest of the religions and finding what is repulsive in them. If a follower of those religions wants to blame something in the religion of these [dialectical theologians], they confront him with the repulsive things in his religion[13] and thereby ward him away from their religion.

Others came to the opinion that the arguments they brought forth to defend things like this were not sufficient to validate them completely so that their adversary's silence would be due to his holding them valid, rather than to his being incapable of countering them by argument. So they were obliged to use things that would compel him to refrain from encounter either from shame and being outmaneuvered or from fear of something abhorrent befalling him.

With others, when the validity of their religion was such they had no doubts about it, [113] they were of the opinion that they would defend it before others, make it attractive, remove suspicion from it, and ward their adversaries away from it by any chance thing. They did not care whether they used falsehood, deceit, slander, or disdain, for they were of the opinion that one of two [kinds of] men would oppose their religion. He would either be an enemy, and it is permissible to use falsehood and deceit to

12. From the way Alfarabi presents this and the following two groups, as contrasted with the way he introduces and concludes groups a and b, these three appear to be subdivisions of b.

13. Literally, "in the religion of those" (*fī milla ulā'ika*)—that is, of those other people.

warn him off and conquer him, as is the case in struggle and warfare.[14] Or he would not be an enemy but one who, due to the weakness of his intellect and discernment, is ignorant of the good fortune for him from this religion; and it is permissible to bring a human being to his good fortune by means of falsehood and deceit, just as that is done with women and children.

14. The terms are *al-jihād* and *al-ḥarb*.

Book of Religion

The translation

This translation is based on the Arabic text edited by Muhsin Mahdi.[1] The numbered sections in the translation correspond to those in the Arabic text and the numerals within square brackets to its page numbers. I have, however, created additional paragraphing within the numbered sections in order to reflect what appear to me to be important steps in Alfarabi's argument. Unfortunately, I did not learn of Lawrence V. Berman's draft translation of this work—*On Religion, Jurisprudence, and Political Science*—until very late in my own efforts and was therefore not able to benefit from it.

The argument of the work

Medieval political philosophy first recommends itself to us because its concerns are so similar to our own. It is rooted in a world affected by revelation and revelation's claim to knowledge about all human matters—knowledge that surpasses the understanding one might acquire through the pursuit of philosophy. Among the medieval political philosophers, those writing within the Islamic tradition are especially insistent upon evaluating the merit of that claim, that is, upon investigating how revela-

1. See *Abū Naṣr al-Fārābī, Kitāb al-Milla wa Nuṣūṣ Ukhrā*, edited, with an introduction and notes, by Muhsin Mahdi (Beirut: Dār al-Mashriq, 1968). The text of the *Book of Religion* is on pp. 41–66. Mahdi's edition is based on the University of Leiden Library Manuscript Cod. Or. 1002 and the summary from the *Akhlāq* 290 manuscript of the Taymūriyya collection in the Egyptian National Library, Cairo.

tion affects unaided human reflection. And they do so in such a manner as to give each side its due or in such a manner as to keep alive the deep tension between the religious and the philosophical approaches. Alfarabi, widely recognized as the founder of medieval Islamic political philosophy, is best known for his inquiries into this issue. Of all his writings, the Book of Religion addresses it most directly and explicitly. It explores the relationship between philosophy and religion, on the one hand, and strives to provide a correct understanding of what that relationship teaches us about political life on the other.

The basic teaching of Alfarabi's *Book of Religion* is that virtuous religion governs a political community and is subordinate to practical, as well as to theoretical, philosophy. Although he speaks of non-virtuous religion, he does so only to distinguish its various species from virtuous religion. Moreover, the size of the political community ruled by virtuous religion does not greatly concern Alfarabi. It may be "a tribe, a city or district, a great nation, or many nations" (section 1). Virtuous religion is by no means limited or diminished insofar as it is subordinated to philosophy. To the contrary, such a subordination vouches for the truth of the opinions and actions its founder prescribes for the people who follow it.

To persuade us of the merit of such a novel view of religion, Alfarabi must bring us to think anew about the meaning of revelation, rulership, and the ruler's craft, as well as about political science. In fact, the *Book of Religion* is really more about political science than it is about religion. Even though the treatise begins with the word "religion" (*al-milla*) and ends with the assertion that a common religion is needed to bring about all that has been set forth heretofore, by far the greater part of the treatise is devoted to a discussion of political science.[2] In only one other of Alfarabi's numerous writings is political science expounded upon at such length, namely, Chapter 5 of the *Enumeration of the Sciences*. Apart from these two, the subject arises in his other writings only in passing, or to illustrate a larger theme.

As was noted in the introduction to the *Enumeration of the Sciences*, Chapter 5, political science as presented there falls short insofar as it is unable to explain everything alluded to in that treatise, especially the con-

2. The treatise consists of 31 sections: sections 1–27 plus sections 14a–d. Of these, sections 1–10 concern religion in general and virtuous religion in particular, while sections 11–27 are devoted to political science, that is, political science simply (section 11 to section 15, paragraph 1) and political science that provides an account of the world consonant with revelation (section 15, paragraph 2, to section 27).

cerns of jurisprudence and theology. Even though the exposition of these two arts follows that of political science, neither the first nor the second account of political science addresses the religious themes central to them. By closing with a discussion of jurisprudence and theology, the *Enumeration of the Sciences* suggests what still needs to be accounted for. Insofar as the Book of Religion opens with a discussion of religion centered in political community, then moves to political science, it seems to represent Alfarabi's reply to this need.

By the way he lets the exposition of the *Book of Religion* unfold, Alfarabi introduces the idea that religion is dependent on philosophy, theoretical as well as practical (see section 5), and that jurisprudence is both a part of political science and dependent on practical philosophy (see section 10). The importance thus attached to practical philosophy obliges Alfarabi to provide at least another account of political science. He does more: as in the *Enumeration of the Sciences*, Chapter 5, so, too, in the *Book of Religion*, he provides the reader with two accounts of political science. Features common to the two accounts in the two works notwithstanding, they are not completely congruent. Though the first account of political science in the *Book of Religion* has just as many deficiencies as the first account of political science in the *Enumeration of the Sciences*, the second account in the *Book of Religion* goes beyond its *Enumeration of the Sciences* counterpart to provide what is needed.[3]

To gain an appreciation of these different accounts of political science and their implications, it is important to look more closely at the formal characteristics of the *Book of Religion*, and especially at the way Alfarabi presents virtuous religion from the outset as highly similar to political science. For example, the criterion used to distinguish virtuous religion from non-virtuous religion—that it strives toward the end of attaining true happiness for the inhabitants of the community—is precisely the one used to distinguish virtuous from non-virtuous political rule (see section 1 with section 14a). There are also incomplete parallels such that the reader is obliged to make the unstated connection: thus the discussion of the way the virtuous religious ruler sets down laws that must be qualified as divine to achieve his purpose closely resembles the discussion of the way

3. As I indicated in the introduction to the *Enumeration of the Sciences*, Chapter 5, the parallel passages between the two works are highly similar. Indeed, the accounts presented in the *Book of Religion* overlap, at times almost word for word, with those set forth in the *Enumeration of the Sciences*. Nonetheless, here, as is so often the case with the writings of Alfarabi, one must be alert to the subtle distinctions between things that are similar.

the virtuous political ruler sets down something like divine laws, even though they are never identified as such, to achieve his end (see sections 1, end, and 4 with sections 5 and 27). Only by explicitly distinguishing the kinds of laws set down by each can one fathom the point of Alfarabi's ever so detailed parallel constructions. Another point of similarity concerns the arrangements to be made so that there can be an orderly succession to the virtuous religious ruler or to the virtuous political ruler (see sections 7–9 with sections 14b–14d). Again, in the opening lines of the treatise, religion is referred to not as creed (*dīn*) or faith (*imān*), but as rulership (*ri'āsa*).[4] And from the very beginning of the treatise, the founder of a religion is referred to as a supreme or first ruler (*ra'īs awwal*) rather than as a prophet. In fact, the term "prophet" almost never occurs in the treatise. The only time it comes close to having its normal significance is in a passage explaining that religion should include opinions about what prophecy is and should provide the populace with descriptions of prophets from earlier times (section 2, but see also section 3).

By describing religion as though it were political in character, Alfarabi approaches the subject from a perspective broader than that normally taken by the worshiper. Generally, the worshiper is content to know how jurisprudence and theology function, what the basic opinions reached in either one are, and how the succession of religious leaders is ordered. Such information is sufficient for instructing others in the religion or for defending the religion from its enemies (section 6). Here, however, Alfarabi goes further and seeks to explain the reasons behind the practices and opinions found in religion as well as to suggest the parallels between religion and other arts, such as political science and philosophy. This broader perspective forces the worshiper to raise new kinds of questions and prods those who refuse to think about religion because they do not take its claims seriously. By making the interconnections between religion and politics so patent, Alfarabi compels his readers to ask more pointed questions about revelation and to investigate how people who claim to have revelation organize the communities they rule.

4. Later, however, religion is said to be almost synonymous with creed (section 4). The term "faith" is, nonetheless, absent from the treatise, and "belief" (*iʿtiqād*) occurs only twice—once to suggest what allows someone to have opinions (section 9) and again, in the plural (*iʿtiqādāt*), in apposition to, and as distinct from, opinions (section 27, end). "Opinions" (*ārā'*) are consistently referred to where the reader would expect to see a reference to beliefs.

At some point, one must query how virtuous religion is to be apprehended by those who look upon it from outside the community or by those who, members of the community or not, wish to grasp better the way it works within the community. Alfarabi's explanation that it is similar to philosophy, even to the extent of admitting the practical and theoretical divisions of philosophy (section 5), shows how it is to be understood. He goes a step further and identifies both the practical and the theoretical divisions within religion as being subordinate to philosophy. The practical is so because its particular actions are classified under the universals of practical philosophy. And the demonstrative proofs of what is claimed in the theoretical part of religion are to be found in theoretical philosophy, even though these things are taken in religion without demonstrative proofs. When these universals are taken over by religion, they become more particular. Indeed, restricted so as to apply to a certain setting or people, they are really particulars. Whether the reasons for the conditions restricting these universals are given in religion or not, they are known in philosophy. That is, philosophy *understands* what is set forth in religion. The same holds for the demonstrations pertaining to the theoretical part of religion: philosophy gives them, whether religion is concerned about them or not.

Practical and theoretical philosophy are, therefore, first mentioned explicitly in the *Book of Religion* simply as means for preserving the opinions and actions passed on by revelation to the first ruler in virtuous religion. That admission leads to the further statement that religion is subordinate to philosophy, practical as well as theoretical. And that statement, in turn, prompts the change in the discussion from religion to political science. (Just as political science is mentioned only in the final section of the first part of the book—that is, section 10—so is religion mentioned only in the final words of the second part of the book—that is, at the end of section 27.) Finally, the discussion of political science leads to the identification of the virtuous kingly craft and the kingly craft linked with revelation—that is, to the substitution of virtue for revelation.

Subsequently, the first discussion of political science is followed—perhaps even replaced—by a second discussion, namely, of political science that is part of philosophy. This political science is able to provide a description of the way the universe is ordered, and its investigation culminates in the assertion that theoretical philosophy alone is able to arrive at an understanding of the truths behind the theoretical opinions put forth in virtuous religion, as well as that religion is a necessary element of any well-ordered political community. To appreciate the significance of this conclusion, it is necessary to learn what Alfarabi has to say about both kinds of political science.

Book of Religion

[43] 1. Religion is opinions and actions, determined and restricted with stipulations and prescribed for a community by their first ruler,[1] who seeks to obtain through their practicing it a specific purpose with respect to them or by means of them.

The community may be a tribe, a city or district, a great nation, or many nations.

If the first ruler is virtuous and his rulership truly virtuous, then in what he prescribes he seeks only to obtain, for himself and for everyone under his rulership, the ultimate happiness that is truly happiness; and that religion will be virtuous religion. If his rulership is ignorant,[2] then in what he prescribes he seeks only to obtain, for himself by means of them, one of the ignorant goods—either necessary good, that is, health and bodily well-being; or wealth; or pleasure; or honor and glory; or conquest—to win that good, be happy with it to the exclusion of them, and make those under his rulership tools he uses to arrive at his purpose and to retain in his possession. Or he seeks to obtain this good for them to the exclusion of himself, or both for himself and them; these two are the most virtuous of the ignorant rulers. If that rulership of his is errant, in that he presumes himself to have virtue and wisdom and those under his rulership pre-

1. A "first ruler" (*ra'īs awwal*) may or may not be first in time, but is always first in rank. That is, he may be the supreme ruler who founds the religion, or the one who succeeds the founder but has full powers as a lawgiver; see below, sections 7–9, 14b, and 18.

2. The different kinds of ignorant cities are described by Alfarabi in the *Political Regime*; see *Alfarabi, The Political Writings: "Political Regime" and Other Texts*, ed. and trans. Charles E. Butterworth (Ithaca: Cornell University Press, forthcoming), sections 93–119.

sume and believe that of him without him being like that [in fact], then he seeks that [44] he and those under his rulership obtain something presumed to be ultimate happiness without it being truly so. If his rulership is deceptive, in that he purposely strives for that[3] without those under his rulership noticing it, then the people under his rulership believe and presume that he has virtue and wisdom; on the surface he seeks in what he prescribes that he and they obtain ultimate happiness, whereas[4] underneath it is that he obtain one of the ignorant goods by means of them.

Now the craft of the virtuous first ruler is kingly and joined with revelation from God. Indeed, he determines the actions and opinions in the virtuous religion by means of revelation. This occurs in one or both of two ways: one is that they are all revealed to him as determined; the second is that he determines them by means of the faculty he acquires from revelation and from the Revealer, may He be exalted, so that the stipulations with which he determines the virtuous opinions and actions are disclosed to him by means of it. Or some come about in the first way and some in the second way. It has already been explained in theoretical science how the revelation of God, may He be exalted, to the human being receiving the revelation comes about and how the faculty acquired from revelation and from the Revealer occurs in a human being.

2. Some of the opinions in virtuous religion are about theoretical things and some about voluntary things.

Among the theoretical are those that describe God, may He be exalted. Then there are some that describe the spiritual beings, their ranks in themselves, their stations in relation to God, may He be exalted, and what each one of them does. Then there are some about the coming into being of the world, as well as some that describe the world, its parts, and the ranks of its parts; how [45] the primary bodies were generated and that some of the primary bodies are the sources of all the other bodies that are gradually generated and pass away; how all the other bodies are generated from the ones that are the sources of bodies and the ranks of these; how the things the world encompasses are linked together and organized and that whatever occurs with respect to them is just and has no injustice; and how each one of them is related to God, may He be exalted, and to the

3. As becomes clear at the end of this sentence, this refers to the deceptive ruler striving to "obtain one of the ignorant goods."

4. Reading *ammā* for *immā* ("either") at 44: 4 and 44: 5.

spiritual beings. Then there are some about the coming into being of the human being and soul occurring in him, as well as about the intellect, its rank in the world, and its station in relation to God and the spiritual beings.[5] Then there are some that describe what prophecy is and what revelation is like and how it comes into being. Then there are some that describe death and the afterlife and, with respect to the afterlife, the happiness to which the most virtuous and the righteous proceed and the misery to which the most depraved and the profligate proceed.

Among the second type of opinions are those that describe the prophets, the most virtuous kings, the righteous rulers, and the leaders of the right way and of truth who succeeded one another in former times; and those that relate what they had in common, what good actions were characteristic of each one, and where their souls and the souls of those who followed and emulated them in cities and nations ended up in the afterlife. There are those that describe the most depraved kings, the profligate rulers exercising authority over the inhabitants of ignorant communities, and the leaders of the errant way who existed in former times; and those that relate what they had in common, what evil actions were characteristic of each one, and where their souls and the souls of those who followed and emulated them in cities and nations ended up in the afterlife. There are those that describe the most virtuous kings, righteous men, and leaders of truth in the present time; and those that mention what they have in common with those who went before and what good actions are characteristic of them. There are those that describe the profligate rulers, the leaders of the errant way, and the inhabitants of ignorant communities in the present time; and those that relate what they have in common with those who went before, what evil actions are characteristic of them, and where their souls will end up in the afterlife.

The descriptions of the things comprised by the opinions of religion ought to be such as to bring the citizens to imagine everything in the city—kings, rulers, and servants; their ranks, the way they are linked together, and the way some yield to others; and everything prescribed to them—so that what is described will be likenesses the citizens will follow in their ranks and actions.

These, then, are the opinions that are in religion. [46]

5. Or, if the pronoun is interpreted as referring to man rather than to the intellect, the phrase would read: "Then there are some about the coming into being of the human being and soul and intellect occurring in him, his rank in the world, and his station in relation to God and the spiritual beings."

3. As for actions, they are, first of all, the actions and speeches by which God is praised and extolled. Then there are those that praise the spiritual beings and the angels. Then there are those that praise the prophets, the most virtuous kings, the righteous rulers, and the leaders of the right way who have gone before. Then there are those that blame the most depraved kings, the profligate[6] rulers, and the leaders of the errant way who went before and that censure their activities. Then there are those that praise the most virtuous kings, the righteous rulers, and the leaders of the right way in this time and that blame those of this time who are their opposites.

Then, after all this, are determining the actions by which the mutual dealings of the inhabitants of the cities are regulated—either regarding what a human being ought to do with respect to himself[7] or regarding how he ought to deal with others—and bringing about cognizance[8] of what justice is with respect to each particular instance of these actions.

This, then, is the sum of what virtuous religion comprises.

4. "Religion" (*milla*) and "creed" (*dīn*) are almost synonymous, as are "law" (*sharīʿa*)[9] and "tradition" (*sunna*). Most often, the latter two signify and apply to the determined actions in the two parts of religion. It may be possible, as well, for the determined opinions to be called "law," so that "law," "religion," and "creed" would be synonymous, given that religion consists of two parts: specifying opinions and determining actions.

The first type of opinions specified in religion is twofold: an opinion designated by its proper name, which customarily signifies it itself; or an

6. Reading *al-fajār*, with Dunlop, instead of *al-fujjār*, with Mahdi; see the review of *Kitāb al-Milla* by D. M. Dunlop in the *Journal of the American Oriental Society* 89 (1969): 801.

7. Or, alternatively, "by himself" (*bi-nafsih*).

8. See *Selected Aphorisms*, note. 5, and also *Enumeration of the Sciences*, Chapter 5, note 3. As in the latter text, the terms here derive from the second form of *ʿarafa*; thus, the question is one of making the inhabitants of the cities aware of, or acquainting them with, something, rather than providing them with knowledge or science about it.

9. Throughout this translation, *sharīʿa* is rendered as "law," the verb *sharraʿa* as "legislate," and the phrase *wāḍiʿ al-sharīʿa* as "lawgiver." The term *nāmūs* does not occur in this work. For *dīn*, see Alfarabi, *Philosophy of Plato*, section 7, in *Alfarabi, The Political Writings: Philosophy of Plato and Aristotle*, trans. Muhsin Mahdi (Ithaca: Cornell University Press, forthcoming). The term *sunna* usually refers to the practices that have come to be traditionally accepted within the religion, because they can be traced back to something the Prophet said or did.

opinion designated by the name of what is similar to it.[10] Thus the determined opinions in the virtuous religion are either the truth or a likeness of the truth. In general, truth is what a human being ascertains, either by himself[11] by means of primary knowledge, or by demonstration. Now any religion in which the first type of opinions does not comprise what a human being can ascertain either from himself[12] or by demonstration and in which there is no likeness of anything he can ascertain in one of these two ways is an errant religion.

5. Thus, virtuous religion is similar to philosophy. Just as philosophy is partly theoretical and partly practical, so it is with religion: the calculative theoretical part is what a human being is not able to do when he knows it, [47] whereas the practical part is what a human being is able to do when he knows it. The practical things in religion are those whose universals are in practical philosophy. That is because the practical things in religion are those universals made determinate by stipulations restricting them, and what is restricted by stipulations is more particular than what is pronounced unqualifiedly without stipulations: for instance, our saying "the human being who is writing" is more particular than our saying "the human being." Therefore, all virtuous laws are subordinate to the universals of practical philosophy. The theoretical opinions that are in religion have their demonstrative proofs in theoretical philosophy and are taken in religion without demonstrative proofs.

Therefore, the two parts of which religion consists are subordinate to philosophy. For something is said to be a part of a science or to be subordinate to a science in one of two ways: either the demonstrative proofs of what is assumed in it without demonstrative proofs occur in that science, or the science comprising the universals is the one that gives the reasons for the particulars subordinate to it. The practical part of philosophy is, therefore, the one that gives the reasons for the stipulations by which actions are made determinate: that for the sake of which they were stipulated and the purpose intended to be obtained by means of those stipula-

10. Alfarabi is referring to the first type of opinions set forth in section 2—those about theoretical things. When speaking of the way humans are brought into being, it is possible to use the proper name for what occurs. When speaking about God or the spiritual beings, similes are used.

11. Or, alternatively, "directly" (*bi-nafsih*).

12. Or, alternatively, "immediately" (*min dhātih*).

tions. Further, if to know something is to know it demonstratively, then this part of philosophy is the one that gives the demonstrative proof for the determined actions that are in virtuous religion. And since it is the theoretical part of philosophy that gives demonstrative proofs for the theoretical part of religion, it is philosophy, then, that gives the demonstrative proofs of what virtuous religion encompasses. Therefore, the kingly craft responsible for what the virtuous religion consists of is subordinate to philosophy.

6. Dialectic yields strong presumption about all or most of what demonstrative proofs yield certainty about, and rhetoric persuades about most of what is not such as to be proven by demonstration or looked into by dialectic. Moreover, virtuous religion is not only for philosophers or only for someone of such a station as to understand what is spoken about only in a philosophic manner. Rather, most people who are taught the opinions of religion and instructed in them and brought to accept its actions are not of such a station—and that is [48] either due to nature or because they are occupied with other things. Yet they are not people who fail to understand generally accepted or persuasive things. For that reason, both dialectic and rhetoric are of major value for verifying the opinions of religion for the citizens and for defending, supporting, and establishing those opinions in their souls, as well as for defending those opinions when someone appears who desires to deceive the followers of the religion by means of argument, lead them into error, and contend against the religion.

7. It may happen accidentally that the first ruler does not determine all of the actions and give an exhaustive account of them, but determines most of them; and with some of those he does determine, it may happen that he does not give an exhaustive account of all their stipulations. On the contrary, for diverse reasons that occur, many actions such as to be determined may remain without determination: death may overtake him and carry him away before he has covered all of them; necessary occupations, such as wars and other things, may keep him from it; or it may be that he only determines actions for each incident and each occurrence he observes or is asked about, at which time he determines, legislates, and establishes a tradition regarding what ought to be done for that kind of incident. Since not everything that can occur does occur in his time or in his country, many things remain that could occur in another time or in another country, each needing a specifically determined action, [49] and

he will have legislated nothing about them. Or else he devotes himself to those actions he presumes or knows to be fundamental, from which someone else can extrapolate the remaining ones: he legislates about the manner and amount of what ought to be done with these and leaves the rest, knowing that it will be possible for someone else to extrapolate them by adopting his intention and following in his footsteps. Or he decides to begin with legislating and determining the actions that are of the greatest efficacy, use, value, and benefit, so that the city will cohere and its affairs will be linked and organized: he legislates about those things alone and leaves the rest for a moment of leisure or so that someone else—a contemporary or a successor—can extrapolate them by following in his footsteps.

8. If, after his death, someone succeeds him who is like him in all respects, then the successor will be the one who determines what the first did not determine. And not only this, but it is also up to him to alter much of what the first had legislated and to determine it in another way, when he knows that this is best for his time—not because the first erred, but because the first made a determination according to what was best for his time and this one makes a determination according to what is best subsequent to the time of the first, this being the kind of thing the first would alter also, were he to observe it. It is the same if the second is followed by a third [50] who is like the second in all respects, and the third by a fourth: it is up to the one who comes after to determine, on his own, what he does not find determined and to alter what his predecessor determined; for, were his predecessor still here, he too would alter what the one who came after altered.

9. Now if one of those righteous leaders who are really kings should pass away and not be succeeded by one who is like him in all respects, it will be necessary—concerning everything done in the cities under the rulership of the predecessor—for the successor to follow in the footsteps of the predecessor with respect to what he determines; he should not do anything differently nor make any alteration, but should let everything the predecessor determined remain the way it was and look into anything that needs to be given a determination and was not declared by the predecessor, inferring and extrapolating itfrom the things the first determined by declaring them.

Thus, the art of jurisprudence would then be requisite. It enables a human being to make a sound determination of each thing the lawgiver did not declare specifically by extrapolating it or inferring it from the things he determined by declaring them and to verify that on the basis of the lawgiver's purpose in the religion he legislated with respect to the nation for which it was legislated. Now this verification is not possible unless his belief in the opinions of that religion is correct and he possesses the virtues that are virtues in that religion. Whoever is like that is a jurist.

10. Since a determination takes place with respect to two things—opinions and actions—the art of jurisprudence must have two parts: a part concerning opinions and a part concerning actions.[13]

Thus, the jurist concerned with [51] actions must have exhaustive knowledge of all the actions the lawgiver has declared specifically. Declaration sometimes takes place through a statement and sometimes through an action of the lawgiver, his action taking the place of saying that a particular thing ought to be done in such and such a way. In addition, the jurist must be cognizant of the laws legislated by the first ruler for a certain moment and then replaced with others he retained so that in his own time the jurist follows in the traces of the latter ones, not the former. The jurist must further be cognizant of the language spoken by the first ruler; of the customary ways in which the people of his time used their language; and of what was used in it to signify something metaphorically, while in reality being the name of something else, so that he does not presume that when the name of one thing was used metaphorically for another thing, the first thing was meant, or presume this thing to have been the other thing. In addition, the jurist must be quite clever at recognizing the meaning intended by an equivocal name in the context in which it is used, as well as at recognizing equivocalness in speech. Also, he must be quite clever at recognizing when an expression is used in an unqualified sense, whereas the intention of the speaker is more restricted; at recognizing when an expression, taken literally, has a restricted meaning, whereas the intention of the speaker is more general; and at recognizing when an expression is used in a restricted, or general, or unqualified sense, whereas the intention of the speaker is what it means literally. He must be cognizant of what is generally accepted and what is customary. In addition, he must have a capacity for grasping similarities and differences in things, as well as a

13. Compare the account of jurisprudence in what follows with that given by Alfarabi in the *Enumeration of the Sciences*, Chapter 5, sections 4-5.

capacity for distinguishing what necessarily follows something from what does not. This comes about through a good natural disposition and through familiarity with the art. He must find out the lawgiver's utterances for everything he legislated in speech and his actions for whatever he legislated by doing it rather than by uttering it: by observing and listening to him, if he is [52] his contemporary and companion, or by having recourse to reports about him; and reports about him are either generally accepted or persuasive, each of these being either written or unwritten.

The jurist concerned with the opinions determined in religion ought already to know what the jurist concerned with practices knows.

Jurisprudence about the practical matters of religion therefore comprises only things that are particulars of the universals encompassed by political science; it is, therefore, a part of political science and subordinate to practical philosophy. And jurisprudence about the [theoretical or] scientific matters of religion comprises either particulars of the universals encompassed by theoretical philosophy or those that are likenesses of things subordinate to theoretical philosophy; it is, therefore, a part of theoretical philosophy and subordinate to it, whereas theoretical science is the source.

11. Political science investigates happiness first of all. It brings about cognizance that happiness is of two types: happiness presumed to be happiness without being such, and happiness that is truly happiness. The latter is the one sought for its own sake; at no time is it sought in order to obtain something else by it; indeed, all other things are sought in order to obtain this one, and when it is obtained, the search is given up; it does not come about in this life, but rather in the next life which is after this one; and it is called ultimate happiness. Examples of what is presumed to be happiness but is not such are affluence, pleasures,[14] honor and being glorified, or anything else sought and acquired in this life that the multitude calls goods. [53]

12. Then it investigates the voluntary actions, ways of life, moral habits, states of character, and dispositions until it gives an exhaustive account of all of them and covers them in detail.

14. Reading *aw al-ladhdhāt*, with Leiden Manuscript Or. 1002, rather than *wa al-ladhdhāt*, with Mahdi.

13. Then it explains that these cannot all be found in one human being nor be done by one human being, but can be done and actually manifest themselves only by being distributed among an association of people.

It explains that when they are distributed among an association of people, the one charged with one kind cannot undertake or do it unless another person assists him by undertaking the kind the latter has been charged with; nor can the latter undertake what he has been charged with unless a third person assists him by undertaking the kind he has been charged with. Moreover, it is not impossible to find a person who cannot undertake the task he has been charged with unless assisted by an association of people, each one of whom undertakes the kind of thing he has been charged with: for example, someone charged with undertaking agriculture cannot complete his task unless a carpenter assists him by preparing wood for the plow, a blacksmith by preparing steel for the plow, and a cowherd by preparing oxen for the yoke.

Thus it explains that it is not possible to reach the purpose of voluntary actions and dispositions, unless they[15] are distributed among a very large association of people—either each assigned to a single individual in the association or each assigned to a single group in the association—so that the groups in the association cooperate, through the actions and dispositions in each, to perfect the purpose of the whole association in the same way that the organs of a human being cooperate, through the capacities in each, to perfect the purpose of the whole body.

[It explains] that it is therefore necessary for the association of people to live close together in a single place. And it enumerates the sorts of associations of people that live close together in a single place: there is a civic association, a national association, and others. [54]

14. Then it distinguishes the ways of life, moral habits, and dispositions that, when practiced in cities or nations, make their dwellings prosper and their inhabitants obtain goods in this life here below, and ultimate happiness in the afterlife; and it sets them apart from those not like that. Only those voluntary actions, ways of life, moral habits, states of character, and dispositions by which ultimate happiness is attained are virtuous; only they are goods; and they are the ones that are truly noble. Any other actions and dispositions are presumed to be goods, virtues, or noble, but are not such—on the contrary, they are truly evils.

15. Literally, "their kinds" or "the kinds of them," (*anwāʿuhā*).

14a. It explains that the things such as to be distributed in a city, in cities, in a nation, or in nations so as to be practiced in common are only brought about by means of a rulership that establishes those actions and dispositions in the city or nation and strives to preserve them for the people so that they do not disappear or become extinct. The rulership by which those ways of life and dispositions are established in a city or nation and preserved for the people cannot come about except by a craft, art, disposition, or faculty that gives rise to the actions by which they are established and preserved. This craft is the craft of the king and the kingly craft, or whatever a human being wants to call it instead of "kingly." And the regime is the work of this craft; that is, it performs the actions by which those ways of life and those dispositions are established in a city or nation and preserved for the people. This craft consists of cognizance of all the actions with which one goes about establishing, first, and preserving afterwards.

The rulership that establishes in a city or nation and preserves for the people the ways of life and dispositions [55] by means of which ultimate happiness is obtained is virtuous rulership. The kingly craft by means of which this rulership comes about is the virtuous kingly craft. The regime that comes into being through this craft is the virtuous regime. The city or nation subject to this regime is the virtuous city and the virtuous nation. The human being who is a part of this city or nation is the virtuous human being.

The rulership, the kingly craft, and the regime that do not aim at obtaining the ultimate happiness that is truly happiness but rather aim at attaining one of the goods particularly characteristic of this world here below—that is, the ones the multitude presumes to be goods—are not virtuous; on the contrary, they are called ignorant rulership, ignorant regime, and ignorant craft: indeed, they are not called "kingly" because, according to the Ancients, kingship was what came about through virtuous kingly craft. The city or the nation subject to the actions and dispositions established in it by the ignorant rulership is called the ignorant city or nation. The human being who is part of this city is called an ignorant human being.[16] This rulership and these cities and nations are divided in several ways; each one of them is called by the name of the purpose it is intent upon among the things presumed to be good: either pleasures, honors, wealth, or something else.

16. Or, perhaps, "a human being in a state of ignorance" (*insān jāhilī*).

Now it is not impossible for a human being who is part of the virtuous city to be living [56] in an ignorant city, voluntarily or involuntarily. That human being is a part foreign to that city, and he may be likened to an animal that happens to have the legs of an animal belonging to an inferior species. Similarly, when someone who is part of an ignorant city lives in a virtuous city, he may be likened to an animal that has the head of an animal belonging to a superior species.[17] For this reason, the most virtuous persons, forced to dwell in ignorant cities due to the non-existence of the virtuous city, need to migrate to the virtuous city, if it happens to come into being at a certain moment.

14b. [Political science explains] that virtuous rulership is of two types: a first rulership and a rulership dependent on it. First rulership is the one that first establishes the virtuous ways of life and dispositions in the city or nation without their having existed among the people before that, and it converts them from the ignorant ways of life to the virtuous ways of life. The person undertaking this rulership is the first ruler.

The rulership dependent on the first is the one that follows in the steps of the first rulership with regard to its actions. The one who undertakes this rulership is called ruler of the tradition and king of the tradition. His rulership is based on an existing tradition.

The first virtuous kingly craft consists of cognizance of all the actions that facilitate establishing the virtuous ways of life and dispositions in cities and nations, preserving them for the people, and guarding and keeping them from the inroad of something from the ignorant ways of life—all of those being sicknesses that befall the virtuous cities. In this sense, it is like the medical craft; for the latter consists of cognizance of all the actions that establish health in a human being, preserve it for him, and guard it from any sickness that might occur. [57]

14c. It is clear that the physician ought to be cognizant that opposites ought to be combated by opposites, be cognizant also that fever is to be combated by chill, and be cognizant further that jaundice should be combated by barley-water or tamarind-water. Of these three, some are more general than others: the most general is that opposites ought to be com-

17. Literally, "another, more venerable species" (*nawʿ ākhar ashraf minh*). Similarly, a literal translation of the contrasting phrase, "inferior species," would be "another species subordinate to it" (*nawʿ ākhar dūnah*).

bated by opposites; the most particular is that jaundice ought to be combated by barley-water; and our saying that "fever is to be combated by chill" is a mean between the more general and the more particular.

However, when the physician cures, he cures the bodies of individuals and of single beings—Zayd's body, for instance, or Amr's body. In curing Zayd's jaundice, he is not content with what he is cognizant of concerning opposites being combated by opposites, nor about jaundice needing to be combated by barley-water unless, with respect to the fever of this Zayd, he has, in addition, cognizance that is more particular than those things he is cognizant of through [the study of] his art. So he investigates whether this jaundice of his ought to be combated by barley-water because his body is cold and moist, or whether barley-water will heal the bodily humor, but not let him perspire, and similar things. If barley-water ought to be drunk, he is not content to be unqualifiedly cognizant of this unless he is cognizant, in addition, of what amount of it ought to be drunk, what consistency what is to be drunk ought to have, at what moment of the day it ought to be drunk, and in which one of Zayd's feverish states it ought to be drunk. So he will have determined that with regard to quantity, quality, and time. Nor is it possible for him to make that determination without observing the sick person, so that his determination accords with what he observes about the state of this sick person, namely, Zayd.

Clearly, he could not have acquired this determination from the books of medicine he studied and was trained on, nor from his ability to be cognizant of the universals and general things set down in medical books, but through another faculty developing from his pursuit of medical practices with respect to the body of one individual after another, from his lengthy observation of the states of sick persons, [58] from the experience acquired by being occupied with curing over a long period of time, and from ministering to each individual. Therefore, the craft of the perfect physician becomes complete, to the point of performing with ease the actions proceeding from that craft, by means of two faculties: one is the ability for unqualified and exhaustive cognizance of the universals that are parts of his art so that nothing escapes him; then there is the faculty that develops in him through the lengthy practice of his art with regard to each individual.

14d. And the first kingly craft is like that. First of all, it comprises universal things. In performing those actions particular to it, the ruler is not content to have comprehensive cognizance of universal things, or the ability to grasp them, unless he has another faculty as well, one acquired through lengthy experience and observation that enables him to determine actions with regard to their quantity, quality, times, and the rest of what actions may be determined by and stipulations placed on them—either with respect to each city, nation, or person, or with respect to an event that occurs or something that happens at particular times. For the actions of the kingly craft are only concerned with particular cities: I mean, this city and that city, this nation and that nation, or this human being and that human being.

Now the faculty by means of which a human being is able to infer the stipulations with which to determine actions with respect to what he observes in each community, each city, each nation,[18] each group, or each person, and with respect to each occurrence in a city, a nation, [59] or a person, is what the Ancients call "prudence." This faculty is not acquired through cognizance of the universals of the art or through exhausting all of them, but through lengthy experience with individual instances.

15. Political science that is a part of philosophy is limited—in what it investigates of the voluntary actions, ways of life, and dispositions, and in the rest of what it investigates—to universals and to giving their patterns. It also brings about cognizance of the patterns for determining particulars: how, by what, and by what extent they ought to be determined. It leaves them undetermined in actuality, because determining in actuality belongs to a faculty other than philosophy and perhaps because the circumstances and occurrences with respect to which determination takes place is infinite and without limitation.

This science has two parts. One part comprises bringing about cognizance of what happiness is—that is, what happiness truly is and what is presumed to be happiness—and enumerating the universal voluntary actions, ways of life, moral habits, states of character, and dispositions that are such as to come about in cities and nations; and it distinguishes the virtuous ones from the non-virtuous. Another part comprises bringing about cognizance of the actions by which virtuous actions and dispositions are established and ordered among the inhabitants of the cities, as well as of the actions by which what has been established among them is preserved for them.

18. Adding *aw ummma umma*, with Leiden Manuscript Or. 1002 and Dunlop, 801.

16. Then it[19] enumerates how many sorts of non-virtuous kingly crafts there are. It also gives the patterns of the actions performed by each one of these kingly crafts in order to obtain its purpose from the inhabitants of the cities under its rulership. It explains that those actions, ways of life, and dispositions that are not virtuous are the sicknesses of virtuous cities and that their ways of life and regimes are the sicknesses of the virtuous kingly craft. The actions, ways of life, and dispositions that are in the non-virtuous cities are the sicknesses of virtuous cities.

17. Then it enumerates how many reasons and tendencies there are because of which the virtuous rulerships and the ways of life of virtuous cities are frequently in danger of being transformed into [60] non-virtuous ways of life and dispositions and how they are transformed into the non-virtuous. It enumerates and brings about cognizance of [a] the actions by which virtuous cities and regimes are restrained so that they not be corrupted and not be transformed into non-virtuous ones and [b] the things by which it is possible to turn them back to health, if they are transformed and become sick.

18. Then it explains that the actions of the first virtuous kingly craft cannot come about completely except through cognizance of the universals of this art; that is, by theoretical philosophy being joined to it and prudence being added to it. Prudence is the faculty acquired through experience arising from long involvement in the actions of the art with respect to single cities and nations and with respect to each single community: it is the ability for excellently inferring the stipulations by which the actions, ways of life, and dispositions are determined with respect to each community, each city, or each nation, either with respect to a short period of time, with respect to a long but limited period of time, or—if possible—with respect to particular times,[20] and for determining them as well with respect to each state that may emerge and each occurrence that may happen in a city, nation, or community. This is what the first virtuous kingly craft consists of. The one dependent on it, whose rulership is based on tradition, does not by nature need philosophy.

19. The subject of all the enumerations, explanations, and so forth in what follows is the "political science that is a part of philosophy" of section 15.

20. This might also mean "or with respect to all time—if possible," for the phrase is quite elusive: *aw bi-ḥasab al-zamān in amkan.*

It explains that what is best and most virtuous in virtuous cities and nations is for their kings and rulers who succeed one another through time to possess the qualifications[21] of the first ruler. It brings about cognizance of [a] how it ought to be worked out so that these kings who succeed one another possess the very same states of virtue and [b] which qualifications are to be sought for in the sons of the city's kings so that if they are found in one of them, it is to be hoped that he will become the same kind of king as the first ruler. In addition, it explains how he ought to be educated, how he is to be raised, and in what way he is to be instructed so that he might become a king completely.

It explains, moreover, that the kings whose rulerships are ignorant need neither the universals of this art nor philosophy. [61] Rather, each one of them can achieve his purpose with respect to the city by means of the experiential faculty he attains through the kind of actions with which he obtains what he is intent upon and arrives at the presumed good that is his purpose, providing he happens to possess a thoroughly deceitful genius capable of inferring what he needs for determining the actions he is to perform and for determining the actions in which he will employ the inhabitants of the city. The craft by which he is a king consists of [a] things attained through experience—either through his own experience or through the experience of some other king who shares in his intention, pursuing his experience or schooling himself in it, and combining that with what he himself has acquired through experience—and [b] matters that he, by the deceitfulness of his genius and cunning, has inferred from the principles he has acquired by experience.[22]

19. Then, after that, it brings about cognizance of the ranks of the things in the world and of the ranks of the beings in general. It begins with the parts of the world that are most inferior, namely, the ones that have no rulership over anything at all and that give rise only to actions used for serving, not to actions used for ruling.

From these, it ascends to the things that rule them without an interme-

21. Literally, "stipulations" (*sharā'iṭ*).

22. This marks the end of the correspondence with the *Enumeration of the Sciences*, Chapter 5, in the account of political science. What follows sets forth what might be termed a "political divine science or theology which keeps one eye on the theoretical sciences and another on human ends and actions." See Muhsin Mahdi, "Science, Philosophy, and Religion in Alfarabi's *Enumeration of the Sciences*," in J. E. Murdoch and E. D. Sylla, eds., *The Cultural Context of Medieval Learning* (Dordrecht: D. Reidel, 1975), pp. 144–45.

diary, namely, the things that rule them directly. It brings about cognizance of their ranks with respect to rulership: what ranks they have; what the extent of their rulership is; that they do not yet have complete rulership; and that their natural traits and faculties are not sufficient for them on that account to have rulership of themselves so that they can dispense with being ruled by others, but that there must necessarily be rulerships over them governing them.

From these, it ascends to the things that rule them directly. It brings about cognizance of their ranks with respect to rulership: what ranks they have; what the extent of their rulership is; that they do not yet have complete rulership; and that their natural traits and faculties are not sufficient for them on that account to have rulership of themselves so that they can dispense [62] with being ruled by others, but that there must necessarily be rulerships over them governing them.

From these, it ascends to the things that rule them directly.[23] It brings about cognizance of their ranks with respect to rulership: what ranks they have; what the extent of their rulership is; and that they are not complete either, except that they are more complete than the rulerships below them. It also brings about cognizance that their natural faculties and traits are not yet sufficient for them to have rulership of themselves so that they have no ruler at all, but that there must necessarily be other rulerships over them governing them.

It ascends, as well, to the things that also rule these directly. With regard to them, it brings about the same cognizance it brought about concerning the former ones.

It does not cease ascending like this from things in lower ranks to things in higher ranks having more complete rulership than those below. In this way, it ascends from the more perfect to more and more perfect beings. It brings about cognizance that whenever it ascends to a higher rank and to a being more perfect in itself and of more perfect rulership, the number of beings in that rank must be fewer and each one of the beings in it must have greater unity in itself and less multiplicity. In addition, it explains the multiplicity and unity that are in a thing.

It does not cease ascending in the perfection of this order from one level of rulership to a more perfect level of rulership until it finally reaches

23. Dunlop, 801, suggests that the immediately preceding passage from "It brings about cognizance . . ." to the end of this sentence "directly" be deleted, believing it to appear as a result of dittography.

a level at which it is impossible for there to be anything but one being—one in number and one in every aspect of oneness. It is impossible as well for there to be a rulership above it; on the contrary, the ruler at that level governs everything below him—it not being at all possible for another to govern him—and rules everything below him. It is not possible [63] for there to be any deficiency in him, not in any way at all; nor is it possible for there to be any perfection more complete than his perfection, nor any existence more excellent than his existence—whereas everything below him has deficiency in some way—and the ranks directly next to him are the most perfect ranks below his level.

20. Then, as it descends, it does not cease [bringing about cognizance that] the beings in each level have more multiplicity and less perfection, until it finally reaches the last beings, namely, the ones that perform servile actions. There is nothing more inferior in existence than these, nor is it at all possible for them to perform ruling actions. The action of the first, the sempiternal one, to whom nothing can be prior, cannot be a servile action at all. And every one of the intermediate ones in the ranks below the first ruler performs ruling actions toward what is below itself by which it serves the first ruler.

In addition, it brings about cognizance of their harmony, of how they are linked together, how they are organized, how their actions are organized, and how they mutually support one another so that despite their multiplicity they might be like one thing. This comes about due to the power with which that one governs them, his governance extending in each of them commensurate with its rank and in accordance with the amount of natural worth a being[24] at that level of existence must have, as well as with the actions that must be entrusted to it for serving, ruling, or doing both.

21. Then it indicates what corresponds to these with respect to the faculties of the human soul.

22. Then it indicates what corresponds to these with respect to the organs of the human body.

24. Reading *mā* ("what," understood here as "a being"), for sense, instead of *man* ("one" or "someone") at 63: 13.

23. Then, it also indicates what corresponds to these with respect to the virtuous city, placing the king and the first ruler in the same station as the deity who is the first governor of the beings and of the world and the classes [of beings] in it.

24. Then, it does not cease going down through the ranks among them until it finally reaches groups within the divisions of the inhabitants of the city whose actions are such that it is not possible for them to rule by means of them, but only to serve, [64] and whose voluntary dispositions are such that it is not possible [for them] to rule by means of them, but only to serve. The groups in the intermediate ranks have actions by means of which they rule what is below them and serve whomever is above them; as they move closer and closer to the level of the king, they are more perfect in traits and actions and, therefore, more perfect in rulership, until the level of the kingly craft is finally reached. It is clear that this is not at all a craft by which a human being can serve; no, it is a craft and a disposition only for ruling.

25. Then, after that, it begins to ascend from the first ranks [in the city], namely, the ranks of serving, to the ranks of rulership directly above them. It does not cease ascending in speech and description from a lower level to a higher level until it finally reaches the level of the king of the city who rules and does not serve.

26. Then it ascends from that level to the level of the spiritual being governing the king who is the first ruler of the virtuous city, namely, the one set down as the trustworthy spirit,[25] and this is the one through which God, may He be exalted, communicates the revelation to the first ruler of the city. Thus it looks into what its level is and which one of the ranks of the spiritual beings it is.

27. Then it does not cease ascending like this in bringing about cognizance of things until it finally reaches the Deity, may His praise be magnified.

25. See the *Quran* 26: 193. In the opening lines of the *Political Regime*, Alfarabi explains that "of the active intellect, it ought to be said that it is the trustworthy spirit and the holy spirit; and it is called by names resembling these two"; see *Political Regime, in Alfarabi, The Political Writings, "Political Regime" and Other Texts*, section 3; for the Arabic text, see Alfarabi, *Kitāb al-Siyāsa al-Madaniyya*, ed. Fauzi M. Najjar, (Beirut: Imprimerie Catholique, 1964), 32: 11–12.

It explains how revelation descends from Him level by level until it reaches the first ruler who thus governs the city or the nation and nations with what revelation from God, may He be exalted, brings, so that the first ruler's governance also extends to every one of the divisions of the city in an orderly manner until it finally reaches the last divisions. It explains this in that God, may He be exalted, is also the governor of the virtuous city, just as He is the governor of the world, [65] and in that His, may He be exalted, governance of the world takes place in one way, whereas His governance of the virtuous city takes place in another way; there is, however, a relation between the two kinds of governing, and there is a relation between the parts of the world and the parts of the virtuous city or nation.

And [it explains that] there must also be harmony, linkage, organization, and mutual support in actions among the parts of the virtuous nation, something similar to the harmony, linkage, organization, and mutual support in actions that exist in the parts of the world due to their natural traits must exist in the divisions of the virtuous nation due to their voluntary traits and dispositions. The Governor of the world places natural traits in the parts of the world by means of which they are made harmonious, organized, linked together, and mutually supportive in actions in such a way that, despite their multiplicity and the multiplicity of their actions, they become like a single thing performing a single action for a single purpose. In the same manner, the governor of the nation must set down and prescribe voluntary traits and dispositions for the souls in the divisions of the nation and city that will bring them to that harmony, linkage of some to others, and mutual support in actions in such a way that, despite the multiplicity of their divisions, the diversity of their ranks, and the multiplicity of their actions, the nation and the nations become like a single thing performing a single action by which a single purpose is obtained. What corresponds to that becomes clear to anyone who contemplates the organs of the human body.

Along with the natural constitutions and instincts that He implanted in the world and its parts, the Governor of the world provided other things that make the existence of the world and its divisions persevere and continue in the way He constituted it for very long periods of time. The governor of the virtuous nation ought to do the very same thing: he ought not to limit himself to the virtuous traits and dispositions that he prescribes for their souls so that they will be made harmonious, linked together, and mutually supportive in actions unless he provides, in addition, other things through which he seeks their perseverance and continuation in the virtues and good things he implanted in them from the outset.

In general, he ought to follow God and pursue [66] the traces of the Governor of the world concerning His provision for the [different] sorts of beings and His governance of their affairs: the natural instincts, constitutions, and traits He set down and implanted in them so that the naturally good things are fully realized in each of the realms according to its level as well as in the totality of the beings. So, too, should he set down in the cities and nations the corresponding arts, and voluntary traits and dispositions, so that the voluntary good things might be fully realized in every single city and nation to the extent that its rank and worth permit, in order that the associations of nations and cities might thereby arrive at happiness in this life and in the afterlife. For the sake of this, the first ruler of the virtuous city must already have thorough cognizance of theoretical philosophy; for he cannot understand anything pertaining to God's, may He be exalted, governance of the world so as to follow it except from that source.

It is clear, in addition, that all of this is impossible unless there is a common religion in the cities that brings together their opinions, beliefs, and actions; that renders their divisions harmonious, linked together, and well ordered; and at that point they will support one another in their actions and assist one another to reach the purpose that is sought after, namely, ultimate happiness.

The Harmonization of the Two Opinions of the Two Sages: Plato the Divine and Aristotle

The translation

This translation is based on the text prepared and edited by Fauzi M. Najjar.[1] Najjar's edition is a marked improvement over the first edition of the work published over a century ago that has served as the basis for all subsequent editions.[2] Dieterici relied on his own edition when he translated the work into German, as did Father Manuel Alonso Alonso for his Spanish and Élie Abdel-Massih for his French translation. Dominique Mallet used an unpublished version of Najjar's edition for his first French translation, and, except for a few modifications and additions, the one accompanying the publication of Najjar's text reproduces that earlier translation.[3] What distinguishes Najjar's edition is

1. See Abū Naṣr al-Fārābī, *L'Harmonie entre les opinions de Platon et d'Aristote*, ed. and trans. Fauzi Mitri Najjar and Dominique Mallet (Damascus: Institut Français de Damas, 1999).

2. See Friedrich Dieterici, *Kitāb al-Jamʿ bayn Ra'yay al-Ḥakīmayn, Aflāṭūn al-Ilāhī wa Arisṭūṭālīs, in Alfārābī's philosophische Abhandlungen aus Londoner, Leidener, und Berliner Handschriften herausgegeben* (Leiden: E. J. Brill, 1890) and Albert N. Nader, *Kitāb al-Jamʿ bayn Ra'yay al-Ḥakīmayn* (Beirut: Imprimerie Catholique, 1960). Nader republished the same text in 1968; several commercial versions of Dieterici's edition have appeared in Cairo from 1907 on.

3. See Friedrich Dieterici, "Die Harmonie zwischen Plato und Aristoteles," in *Alfārābī's philosophische Abhandlungen aus dem Arabischen übersetzt* (Leiden: E. J. Brill, 1892); Fr. Manuel Alonso Alonso, "Concordia entre el divino Platon y el sabio Aristoteles," *Pensamiento* 25 (1969); Élie Abel-Massih, "Livre de concordance entre les opinions des deux sages: le divin Platon et Aristote," *MELTO, Recherches orientales* 2 (1969), Université Saint-

that his draws not only on the two manuscripts on which the first edition was based, but on nine others as well.[4] Of special significance is his reliance on the very accurate manuscript no. 1970 from the Central Library in Diyarbekir, Turkey. In addition to being the most accurate of all the manuscripts, it is also the oldest and the most complete. Moreover, Najjar has complemented the readings of the Diyarbekir manuscript by recourse to another two Turkish manuscripts, plus two others from the Princeton University Library collection, as well as four manuscripts from the Central Library of Teheran University.[5] The text now at our disposition seems, therefore, most reliable.

Because of the importance of the Diyarbekir manuscript for the establishment of the text, the numbers of its pages are indicated in square brackets in this translation. The division of the text into paragraphs and sentences reflects our understanding of the argument, as do the titles assigned the different parts of the text. These parts are signaled in the Diyarbekir manuscript, however, by letters in thick pen strokes. The translation presented here was begun by Fauzi M. Najjar and then completed and revised by Charles E. Butterworth, who also added the notes.[6]

Esprit, Kaslik, Lebanon; and Dominique Mallet, "L'harmonie entre les opinions des deux sages, le divin Platon et Aristote," in *Deux traités philosophiques* (Damascus: Institut Français de Damas, 1989).

4. The first edition relied on British Museum, no. 7518; and Berlin, Petermann II, no. 578.

5. Najjar has used the two manuscripts already noted, plus Diyarbekir Central Library, no. 1970; Princeton University Library, Garrett, no. 794; Princeton University Library, Yahuda, no. 605; Istanbul Köprülü Library, Fazil Ahmet Pasha, no. 347; Istanbul Topkapi Saray Library, Emanet Hazinesi, no. 1730; University of Teheran, Central Library, Mishkāt, no. 253; University of Teheran, Central Library, Mishkāt, no. 240; University of Teheran, Central Library, Dānishkadah, No. 242; and University of Teheran, Central Library, Dānishkadah Adabiyyāt, no. 5179. For details concerning all of the manuscripts, see Najjar, "Introduction au texte arabe," in Najjar and Mallet, *L'Harmonie entre les opinions de Platon et d'Aristote*, pp. 45–51

6. In this respect, Fauzi Najjar deserves equal billing, not to mention my deepest gratitude, as collaborator or co-author of this translation. Special thanks are also due to Paul Walker for his helpful suggestions with respect to difficulties in the text, and to Dominique Mallet, whose notes to his French translation have been most instructive. Miriam Galston's unpublished translation of this work, prepared for Harvard University students of Arabic 249 almost three decades ago, escaped my attention until I chanced upon it while correcting the copy-edited version of the present translation. Consequently, I could make no use of her work.

The argument of the work

From everything that we have read by Alfarabi thus far—that is, from the *Selected Aphorisms* through the *Enumeration of the Sciences,* Chapter 5, and the *Book of Religion*—with respect to politics, generally, but also with respect to the relationship he discerns between the philosophy of the ancients and religion as set forth in the new revelation brought by the Prophet Muhammad, one might object that he relies too much on a presumption of harmony and agreement between Plato and Aristotle on these matters. Indeed, in all of these works, he presents Plato and Aristotle as though they set forth one and the same teaching. We know, however, that the two differed about many minor and not-so-minor questions. This issue is addressed in the treatise before us, the highly enigmatic *Harmonization.* Here, Alfarabi, desirous of putting an end to the disputes and discord among his contemporaries about the disagreement they claim to discern between "the two eminent and distinguished sages, Plato and Aristotle," sets out to show that their opinions are in agreement, to "remove doubt and suspicion from the hearts of those who look into their books," and to "explain the places of uncertainty and the sources of doubt in their treatises."

These goals, set forth in the opening words of the treatise, are surely most appealing. But do they not too readily discount or ignore simple facts manifest to any student of Plato and Aristotle? Almost as though it were an objection he had anticipated, Alfarabi's final observation at the beginning of the treatise affirms that such agreement or harmonization is "among the most important [things] to be intent upon explaining and among the most beneficial to wish to expound upon and to elucidate." Still, what is important and beneficial is not always the same as what is true. And one sign of the possibility that there are differences between Plato and Aristotle not to be ignored is the way Alfarabi distinguishes the one from the other in the very title of his work on harmonization, that is, by calling Plato "divine."

Nor does Alfarabi seek to argue here that the differences between the two can all be explained away. He focuses, instead, on showing that they do not disagree about fundamentals. That is in keeping with the way he closes the *Attainment of Happiness,* admonishing the reader: "So let it be clear to you that their [that is, Plato's and Aristotle's] purpose is the same in what they presented and that they intended to present one and the same philosophy."

Even this overstates the case. In the treatise following the *Attainment*, namely, the *Philosophy of Plato*, Alfarabi presents Plato's philosophical quest as beginning with the inquiry into human perfection and thus human happiness. It is a quest that leads him to investigate what kinds of knowledge make human beings happy and perfect and how such knowledge might be obtained. At first, the quest takes him through the practical arts and the knowledge that is generally accepted among humans. Finding these inadequate, he also investigates the qualities of soul praised by human beings and eventually hits upon the importance of love and friendship. These somehow lead him to philosophy and statesmanship, to the quest for what is truly good, and then to the discovery of the importance of conversation for instruction. At that point, he returns from this high point to the city and to the recognition that true philosophy and statesmanship are not valued there. Indeed, Alfarabi's Plato constantly moves between investigations that take him away from the city and the concerns of the city then bring him back to the city and its needs. He finds repeatedly that what is true, just, and good is not appreciated in the city. But only after the investigation that leads him to recognize what a truly just city might be, namely, "a city that will not lack anything that leads its citizens to happiness" (*Philosophy of Plato*, section 31)—an investigation that "is to be found in his book the *Republic*," says Alfarabi (section 32)—does Plato investigate "the divine and natural beings as they are perceived by the intellect and known by means of that science" (section 33). In other words, Alfarabi's Plato moves from the city, to the world of nature and to the principles on which it rests, then back to the city—not, like Plato's Socrates, for example, from reflection on nature to one on political and human things.

Alfarabi's Aristotle does not proceed in the same manner. It is not clear, moreover, that his philosophy is the same as that of Alfarabi's Plato. Whereas the philosophy of his Plato starts from, and constantly returns to, the human things, that of his Aristotle starts from the principles on which human things are based and moves from them to the principles governing the universe. Though he returns from time to time to speak about human affairs, Alfarabi's Aristotle is much more rooted in natural investigations and in what natural things stand on—in the metaphysical. The difference between the two is stated clearly at the outset of the *Philosophy of Aristotle*:

> Aristotle sees the perfection of man as Plato sees it and more. However, because man's perfection is not self-evident or easy to explain by a demon-

stration leading to certainty, he saw fit to start from a position anterior to that from which Plato had started.

In other words, and this is still in keeping with the main thrust of the *Harmonization,* though there is a difference between the two, it is a mere procedural difference, one rooted in Aristotle's desire to posit certain premises or to lay bare certain suppositions that Plato had neglected. At the end of the exposition, however, Alfarabi lets slip—if it is accurate to say that Alfarabi ever lets anything slip—the following:

> It has become evident that the knowledge that he [Aristotle] investigated at the outset just because he loved to do so, and inspected for the sake of explaining the truth about the above-mentioned pursuits, has turned out to be necessary for acquiring the intellect for the sake of which man is made.

Not gentle buttressing of Plato, then, nor even an attempt to provide the necessary antecedents for Plato's investigation—which is supposed to be one and the same as his—but a different tack entirely, one pursued out of simple love of learning, prompts Aristotle's difference.

Though this is a more accurate image of the way the philosophical pursuits of Plato and Aristotle appear to us, there is still a sense in which those pursuits appear to be one and the same. One way to see this is to consider what Alfarabi has to say about Plato and Aristotle, though mentioning them by name only in passing, in the *Selected Aphorisms,* a work that overlaps in its themes as well as in its literal phrases with the *Attainment.* Alfarabi calls upon Plato and Aristotle in the *Aphorisms* to identify the political order that will achieve human happiness. The individual who succeeds in understanding how a political community can be well-ordered—whether this person is a statesman or a king—will do for the citizens what the physician does for individual sick persons and will accomplish for the citizens who follow his rules what the prophet accomplishes for those who follow his. To attain such an understanding, one must first be fully acquainted with the soul as well as with political life. This is why such a patently political treatise contains two long discussions of the soul (Aphs. 6–21 and 33–56) as well as an investigation of the sound and erroneous opinions with respect to the principles of being and to happiness (Aphs. 68–87).

Whereas both discussions of the soul are very similar to the *Nico-*

machean Ethics, the investigation centered on opinions is couched in terms such as to call Plato's Socrates to mind. Moreover, the second discussion of the soul is followed by an inquiry into the virtuous city (Aphs. 57–67) that vividly calls to mind discussions raised in Plato's *Republic*. Just as the first moral digression is followed by a series of aphorisms that bring political questions into sharper focus, so is the second moral digression followed by a set of politically-oriented aphorisms. It seems, then, that Aristotle's moral concerns permit one to grasp Plato's political concerns more fully. Differently stated, the treatise's moral teaching, grounded in Aristotelian principles, provides the driving force for its political teaching—one grounded in Platonic principles. In this sense, Aristotle seems to provide the groundwork for Plato's loftier queries. Though subsequent to Plato in time, he is necessary for the fuller understanding of Plato's thought.

Another way to learn about the relationship between these two all-important philosophic predecessors—perhaps even to come to view them as nearly identical in their intentions, if not in their procedures—is to consider what Alfarabi has to say about them in the *Harmonization*. In turning to it, however, one cannot help but notice immediately how the style of this work distinguishes it from the preceding treatises. Here the language is much more florid, much richer and more colorful, than it is in these other writings. Moreover, in a number of instances, the arguments are explicitly based on an appeal to common opinion; and for support, they sometimes refer to what everyone says (see, for example, section 4). Alfarabi does, to be sure, gently correct common opinion, but he does so far less often here than in his other works. Finally, and perhaps most striking, there is a reliance here on works not usually cited. We learn, for instance, of an exchange of letters between Plato and Aristotle (section 15), as well as of a little-known letter purportedly written by Aristotle to Alexander (section 13). And at the end of the treatise, Alfarabi finds it necessary to rely not only on the most unusual work entitled the *Theology of Aristotle*, which he must surely have known to be spurious, but also upon an equally suspect letter that Aristotle is supposed to have written to the mother of Alexander. It appears that the goal of bringing Aristotle and Plato into harmony—really, of bringing Aristotle's teaching into closer alignment with Plato's—is of such importance that all means are warranted.

The alleged differences between Plato and Aristotle are accounted for in terms of the different goals each had or the different circumstances that surrounded their writing, more than they are shown to be without foundation. Differently stated, Alfarabi harmonizes the two opinions of these two sages by showing why people mistake other kinds of differences between the two for intellectual differences. Thus he never denies that they acted in different ways or lived in dissimilar manners. He insists, rather, that despite such differences or divergences—which are to be attributed at one time to a difference in the natural powers or faculties of each (section 11) and at another to a difference in the goal each set for himself (sections 19–20 with section 17)—their opinions do not diverge. The point, however, is that Alfarabi insists upon or asserts the existence of such agreement; he does not prove it.

The differences others discern in the writing of Plato as compared to that of Aristotle are not denied; indeed, Alfarabi would have been foolhardy to attempt to do so. He argues, instead, that they are similar in that the writing of each is obscure and difficult to follow, as well as that the different style pursued by the one and the other was dictated by different circumstances (section 16). He follows the same procedure with respect to the question of the approach each took to definitions and to the way each used syllogisms. According to Alfarabi, the minor differences that can ultimately be identified between Plato and Aristotle with respect to these issues are due more to the differences in their pursuits than to a difference in method (section 23). Most of the other differences can be attributed to errors made by those who attempted to comment on their works (section 25). Here, as throughout the treatise, Alfarabi demonstrates an enviable familiarity with the writings of the two sages that shows how deep an understanding he had of the teaching of each.

An observant reader will note, nonetheless, that the argument or exposition as a whole is tendentious. Indeed, Alfarabi scolds and obscures here more than he elucidates and enlightens. Stated differently, his attempt to prove fundamental agreement between Plato and Aristotle is at times as stilted as the language he uses in the process. Why, then, does he pursue such a task? Why is it important and beneficial to have a firm opinion about the basic agreement between these two philosophers? Why can differences between them not be acknowledged as a natural consequence of two exceptionally thoughtful human beings attempting to achieve an understanding of difficult questions?

The only answer that offers itself, one that serves as a guide of sorts to deeper study of the treatise, is found in the opening sections: to admit disagreement between Plato and Aristotle is to call the whole enterprise of philosophy into question. Because philosophy offers the sole viable correction to the exaggerations and sophistical tricks of those who oppose its explanations, it along with its two founders must be defended. Still, as noted above, there is another aspect of the defense that must also be reflected upon due to the way it nuances this response: throughout the *Harmonization,* Alfarabi is more intent on showing that Aristotle agrees with Plato—with bringing Aristotle's teaching into harmony with Plato's—than on proving that Plato's teaching agrees with Aristotle's. Though one might explain such a procedure on historical grounds, noting that Aristotle comes later and must thus be shown to have followed his predecessor, that is not sufficient. The point remains that of the two, Plato alone is identified as "divine." His teaching is closer to what is readily accepted in the community, and a defense of philosophy for the community must therefore be couched in terms that show all of philosophy to follow upon and develop his procedures and explanations.

The Harmonization of the Two Opinions of the Two Sages: Plato the Divine and Aristole

[INTRODUCTION: WHAT THE PEOPLE OF OUR TIME CLAIM]

1. [1b] I see most of the people of our time delving into and disputing over whether the world is generated or eternal. They claim that there is disagreement between the two eminent and distinguished sages, Plato and Aristotle, concerning: the proof [of the existence] of the First Innovator; the causes[1] existing due to Him; the issue of the soul and the intellect; recompense for good and evil actions; and many political, moral, and logical issues. So I want to embark in this treatise of mine upon a harmonization of the two opinions of both of them and an explanation of what the tenor of their arguments signifies in order to make the agreement between the beliefs of both apparent, to remove doubt and suspicion from the hearts of those who look into their books, and to explain the places of uncertainty[2] and the sources of doubt in their treatises. For that is among the most important [things] to be intent upon explaining and among the most beneficial to wish to expound upon and to elucidate.

2. Now the definition of philosophy and what it consists in are that it is knowledge of existing things insofar as they are existent.[3] These two sages

1. The term is *asbāb* (sing., *sabab*) and will usually be translated in what follows as "reasons" or "reason"; see section 5.

2. Literally, "the topics of presumptions" (*mawāḍiʿ al-ẓunūn*).

3. For Plato, see *Republic*, 5.473c-6.503b, esp. 5.475b-c, 480a, and 6.485b; also 7.521c,

are the fountainheads of philosophy, the originators of its beginnings and fundamentals, the fulfillers of its ends and branches. We depend upon them for what is minor and what is major with respect to it; we turn to them for what is slight and what is important with respect to it. Whatever they produce in any of its disciplines is the dependable fundamental, free from blemish and turbidity. Tongues have proclaimed this, and intellects have testified to it—if not all, then most of those possessing pure hearts and lucid minds.

Now a belief is true and accurate when it corresponds to the way the thing expressed is. Thus the difference between the two statements of these two sages [2a] with respect to many of the disciplines[4] of philosophy is inevitably due to one of three things: either this definition disclosing what philosophy consists in is not correct, or the opinion and belief of all or most people concerning the philosophizing of these two Ancients is fatuous and spurious, or there is some deficiency in the cognition of those who presume that there is a difference between the arguments of these two regarding these fundamentals.

3. The definition is correct and corresponds to the meaning of the art of philosophy. This becomes evident from [considering] the particulars of this art by means of induction. That is, the subject matters of the sciences can only be divine, natural, political, mathematical, or logical. And the art of philosophy is the one that infers and extrapolates all of these so that there is nothing among the existing things of this world that philosophy does not have access to, a purpose in, and knowledge of, to the extent humanly possible.

The method of division[5] expounds and elucidates what we have mentioned, and it is the one the sage Plato prefers. Indeed, he who uses divi-

525b, 527b, and 10.611e. For Aristotle, see *Metaphysics*, 4.1.1003a20-3.1005b34 and 11.2.1060b31-32. Also, the term translated as "knowledge" here is *ʿilm*, just as *maʿrifa* will be translated as "cognition"; see *Selected Aphorisms*, note 5. Note that instead of "what it [that is, philosophy] consists in" in this sentence and "what philosophy consists in" in the next paragraph, a more literal translation would be "its whatness" or even "its quiddity" in the first case and "the whatness of philosophy" or even "the quiddity of philosophy" in the second; the Arabic term is *māhiyyātuhā*.

4. Literally, "kinds" (*anwāʿ*).

5. In the Platonic dialogues, Socrates invariably seeks to understand the meaning of a particular term by asking his interlocutor about its parts. See, for example, his investigation of courage in the *Laches*, 185b-e and 189d-192b; as well as his investigation of piety in the *Euthyphro*, 5c-d. In the *Sophist*, the Eleatic Stranger almost makes a mockery of this procedure; see 258b–262a.

sion wishes to let none of the existing things elude him. Had Plato not pursued this [method], the sage Aristotle would have had to originate and pursue it. However, when he found that the sage Plato had mastered, become skillful in, explained, and elucidated it, Aristotle toiled mightily and struggled greatly to originate the method of the syllogism and embarked upon explaining and refining it so as to use it in each and every part necessitated by division that he might be a successor who completes and an assistant of good counsel.

To anyone trained in the science of literature—that is, logic—who then embarks upon the science of natural and of divine things [2b] and studies the books of these two sages, the accuracy of what we say will become evident. He will find that both have been intent upon putting in writing the sciences about the existing things of the world and have struggled to elucidate their conditions as they really are without being intent upon invention, innovation, exaggeration, embellishment, or fastidiousness, but rather upon giving each its due and share as much as is at all possible. This being the case, the definition of philosophy stated, namely, that it is knowledge of existing things insofar as they are existent, is a correct definition that discloses the essence of being and indicates what it is.

4. That the opinion and belief of all or most about these two sages being highly regarded [individuals] and prominent leaders in this art are fatuous and spurious is far from what intellect accepts and defers to. Indeed, existence testifies to the contrary. We know for certain that there is no proof more powerful, more persuasive, or more masterful than the testimonies of various cognitions to the same thing and the unanimous agreement of many intellects about it. For intellect, according to everyone, is proof. Precisely because someone endowed with intellect sometimes imagines one thing after another different from the way it really is, owing to the similarities of the signs signifying its condition, it is necessary to have the agreement of many diverse intellects. Once they agree, there is no proof more powerful and no certainty more masterful than that.

Conversely, do not let yourself be misled by the existence of many creatures having spurious opinions. For when [members of] a community slavishly adhere to a single opinion and defer to a leader to precede them and direct them in what they agree upon, they are as a single intellect. And, as we have already mentioned, a single intellect sometimes errs about one thing, especially if it does not frequently ponder [3a] the opinion it believes, often probe into it, or look into it with a scrutinizing and critical eye. To accept something on mere presumption and, likewise, to fail to investigate it may cover over, blind, and lead astray.

But when various intellects come to be in agreement—after reflecting on, pondering, investigating, examining, criticizing, disputing, and bringing up opposing passages—there will then be nothing more correct than what they believe in, testify to, and agree upon. And we find the various tongues unrestrained about the eminence of these two sages in philosophy. They are cited as examples, and high consideration is bestowed on them. They are described as the ultimate in profound wisdom, subtle knowledge, remarkable inferences, and fathoming the delicate meanings that lead to purity and truth in everything.

5. This being the case, what remains is that there is deficiency in the cognition of those who presume that the two of them differ about fundamentals. You ought to know that there is no presumption, erroneous or apposite, without there being a reason leading to and provoking it. And we shall explain in this place some of the reasons leading to the presumption that there is a difference about fundamentals between the two sages. Then we will follow that by a harmonization of the two opinions of both of them.

6. We say then: A judgment about the whole based on [considering] some particulars by means of an induction is so convincing to [human] nature that it is not disavowed, nor is it possible to abstain from it or free oneself from it with respect to (a) sciences, opinions, and beliefs; (b) the reasons for the nomoi and the laws;[6] or, (c) likewise, the civic ways of life and associations. With respect to natural things, [3b] this is like our judging that all stones sink in water and that all plants burn in fire, although some [plants] may not burn and although some stones may float; or that the mass of the universe is finite, although it may be infinite. With respect to legal matters, it is like [our judging] that whoever is observed doing good in most instances is a just and accurate witness in many such instances. With respect to [civic] associations, it is

6. The terms are *nāwāmīs* (sing., *nāmūs*) and *sharā'i'* (sing., *sharī'a*). While the first signifies conventional laws, the second evokes the notion of divine law, especially the revealed law of Islam. Thus the term translated as "legal matters" in the sentence after the next is *shar'iyyāt*.

like the trust and confidence we find in our souls for someone whom we have often seen behave uprightly, without having observed him in all instances.

7. Now the matter in question, as we have described it, is such that it seizes and dominates one's nature. Moreover, an apparent difference has been found between Plato and Aristotle with respect to ways of life, actions, and many statements. How, then, to refrain from conjecturing and judging that there is a universal difference between them, given the prevailing conjecture that both action and speech follow belief—particularly when there has been no challenge to, or hesitation about, it with the passing of time?

[CHAPTER ONE: ABOUT THEIR DIVERGENT ACTIONS AND DIFFERENT WAYS OF LIFE]

8. Among their divergent actions and different ways of life is Plato's withdrawal from most worldly concerns,[7] rejection of them, warning against them in many of his statements, and predilection for shunning them. In contrast, Aristotle's involvement with what Plato had fled was such that he possessed much property, married, procreated, served Alexander [the Great] as a vizier, and embraced worldly concerns—none of which is concealed from anyone who carefully studies the books telling about the Ancients. On the surface, this divergence compels the presumption and the assurance that there is a difference between their two beliefs about [4a] the issue of the two abodes.[8]

9. The matter is not like that in truth. For it is Plato who has put in writing [an account of] political regimes and how to improve them, explained the just ways of life and human civic association, expounded their virtues, and made apparent the corruption resulting from the actions of those who flee civic association and reject mutual cooperation. His treatises dealing with what we have mentioned are well known and have been studied by various nations from his time to this age of ours. However, he was of the opinion that making the soul upright is the most worthwhile thing for a

7. Literally, "worldly reasons" (*al-asbāb al-dunyawiyya*). The same expression occurs in the next sentence.

8. That is, this life and the hereafter.

human being to begin with and that only after having mastered making it just and upright is one to go on to making others upright. But when he did not find the power in himself to accomplish that, he dedicated his days to his most important obligations, resolving that once he accomplished the most important and worthwhile he would then turn his attention to the closer and nearer, just as he recommended in his treatises on politics and ethics.[9]

10. Aristotle proceeded in a manner similar to Plato in his political statements and epistles. But when he turned to the issue of his own soul, he sensed that he possessed the power, liberality, persistence, broad moral character, and perfection to enable him to make it upright and still have leisure to cooperate [with others] and enjoy many political relations.[10]

11. Accordingly, he who reflects upon these conditions will know that there is no difference between the two opinions and the two beliefs. The reason for the divergence that occurs is nothing other than a deficiency in the natural powers of the one and an excess in those of the other—as

9. For a fuller account of how Alfarabi understands Plato's life and philosophical pursuits, see *Philosophy of Plato* in *Alfarabi, The Political Writings: Philosophy of Plato and Aristotle*, trans. Muhsin Mahdi (Ithaca: Cornell University Press, forthcoming), especially sections 21–38; for the Arabic text, see *Alfarabius, de Platonis Philosophia (Falsafat Aflāṭūn)*, ed. Franz Rosenthal and Richard Walzer (London: Warburg Institute, 1943).

Plato was born in Athens in 427 B.C.E. Having witnessed the end of the Peloponnesian war and the fall of the Athenian democracy in 404, then its restoration, along with the subsequent trial and execution of Socrates in 399, he left Athens for a period of a dozen years. After spending some time in Sicily with Dion in 387, he returned to Athens and founded the Academy. There he remained until his death in 347, except for two brief excursions to Sicily in 367 and 362—the first time at the behest of Dion and the second time at the urging of his nephew, Dionysius the younger. Both trips had as their goal the instruction of Dionysius the younger, Plato's hope being that he might learn to rule in accordance with philosophy. See David Grene, *Man in His Pride: A Study in the Political Philosophy of Thucydides and Plato* (Chicago: University of Chicago Press, 1950), pp. 97–101 and 164–76; also Plato, *Seventh Letter*, 324a–b, 326b–327b, 328b–330b, 337e–341a, and 345c–352a.

10. Literally, "political reasons" (*al-asbāb al-madaniyya*). For another account of how Alfarabi understands Aristotle's relation to Plato, see *Philosophy of Aristotle* in *Alfarabi, The Political Writings: Philosophy of Plato and Aristotle*, especially sections 1–14.

Aristotle was born in Stagira, in northern Greece, in 384 B.C.E. When he was seventeen, he went to Athens, where he pursued studies at Plato's Academy for the next twenty years. Then, for reasons that are not fully known, he left Athens in 347 and went to Assos in Asia Minor. While there, he became friendly with the ruler, Hermias of Atarneus, and

inevitably happens between any two human beings. For most people may know what is preferable, more correct, and more worthwhile without perhaps having the aptitude for it or being capable of [achieving] it; or they may have an aptitude for some [worthy things] [4b] and lack the strength for others.

[CHAPTER TWO: ON THE DIVERGENCE IN THEIR PROCEDURES IN PUTTING THE SCIENCES IN WRITING]

12. Another instance is the divergence in their procedures in putting the sciences in writing and composing books and treatises. In his earlier days, Plato used to refrain from putting any of the sciences in writing and depositing them in the interior of books instead of in unsullied breasts and congenial intellects. When he became fearful of becoming negligent and forgetful as well as of losing what he had inferred, discovered by thinking, and achieved in areas where his knowledge and wisdom had been established and developed, he resorted to allegories and riddles. He intended thereby to put in writing his knowledge and wisdom according to an approach that would let them be known only to the deserving, to those worthy of comprehending them because of research, investigation, examination, struggle, study, and genuine inclination.[11] In contrast, Aristotle's procedure is to clarify, elucidate, put in writing, order, communicate, uncover, and explain, making full use of any of these he finds an approach to.

These two approaches are apparently divergent. But the modes of abstruseness, obscurity, and complexity in Aristotle's procedure, despite his apparent intention to explain and elucidate, will not be concealed from anyone who carefully investigates his scientific teachings,[12] studies his books, and perseveres with them.

---

eventually married Hermias's niece, Pythias. In 343, he accepted Philip's invitation to Macedonia either to become the tutor of his son Alexander or to set up a school for the sons of the aristocracy. About eight years later, he returned to Athens and founded the Lyceum. Then, following Alexander's death in 323, Aristotle fled Athens for Chalcis in Euboea to escape the anti-Macedonian disturbances and died there in 322. For more details, see *Aristotle, The Politics*, trans. Carnes Lord (Chicago: University of Chicago Press, 1984), pp. 2–6 and *Dictionnaire des philosophes antiques*, ed. Richard Goulet et al. (Paris: CNRS Éditions, 1994), article 414, "Aristote de Stagire," vol. 1, pp. 413–590.

11. See section 61, and Alfarabi, *Philosophy of Plato*, section 28. See also Plato, *Seventh Letter*, 341b-e; and *Phaedrus*, 274c–275b and 275d-e.

12. Literally, "sciences" (*ʿulūm*).

13. One finds in his statements, for example, that he omits the necessary premise from many of the syllogisms he adduces in physics, theology, and ethics; the locations of these [omissions] have been indicated by the commentators. Moreover, he omits many conclusions. Again, he omits one of a pair [of terms], limiting himself to a single one, as [5a] in his "Letter to Alexander about the Constitutions of Particular Cities"[13] when he says: "He who chooses justice in mutual association deserves to be distinguished by the governor of the city in punishment." Complete, this statement is like this: "He who prefers to choose justice over injustice deserves to be distinguished by the governor of the city in punishment and reward." That is, he who prefers justice deserves to be rewarded just as he who prefers injustice deserves to be punished. Another instance is his mentioning two premises of a certain syllogism and following them with the conclusion of another syllogism. Another is his mentioning certain premises and following them with the conclusion of the concomitants of those premises, as he has done in the *Prior Analytics* where he mentions that the parts of a substance are substances.[14]

14. Another instance is his speaking at length when enumerating the particulars of something obvious to display his unsparing and strenuous effort at thoroughness, then passing over the obscure without speaking about it at length nor defining it sufficiently.

15. Another instance is the organization, order, and arrangement of his scientific books such that one presumes it to be a natural characteristic of his that he cannot alter. But if his letters are reflected on, the speech in

13. See Józef Bielawski and Marian Plezia, *Lettre d'Aristote à Alexandre sur la politique envers les cités* (Archiwum Filologiczne, XXV; Warsaw: Polskiej Akademii Nauk, 1970).The work contains the Arabic text of the letter (pp. 27–54) with a French translation (pp. 57–73) and an extensive commentary (pp. 75–106). Bielawski and Plezia point to the numerous other citations of the letter in Greek, Latin, and Arabic sources, as well as to parallels between it and other writings by Aristotle. Examining the letter's historical, doctrinal, and literary conformity to the putative setting and to Aristotle's other works, they conclude that the Arabic text is "an extract of an authentic missive sent by Aristotle to Alexander in 330" and that "it would be a master-piece of literary and psychological art—if it were not the authentic voice of Aristotle" (see pp. 9, 15–17, and esp. 163–66; also 149–50). Still, despite numerous juxtapositions of double terms or pairs in the letter, there is nothing in it similar to the phrase cited by Alfarabi.

14. Literally, the reference is to the "Book of the Syllogism" (*Kitāb al-Qiyās*), which, unless otherwise noted, is the way Alfarabi refers to the *Prior Analytics* in the rest of this treatise. See Aristotle, *Prior Analytics*, 1.32.47a24-27; and also *Topics*, 8.11.162a15.

them will be found to be arrayed and organized according to arrangements and orders differing from what is in those books. It is sufficient for us to mention his famous[15] letter to Plato in response to what Plato had written in reproaching him for putting books in writing, ordering the sciences, and bringing this out in complete and exhaustive compositions. In this letter to Plato, he states explicitly: "Although I have put these sciences and their well-guarded and sparingly-revealed maxims in writing, I have nevertheless ordered them in such a manner that only those suited for them will get them, and I expressed them in an idiom that only those adept in them[16] will comprehend."[17]

16. Thus, it appears from what we have described that what initially leads [people] to conjecture that their pursuits diverge [5b] is in fact a matter of two apparently different circumstances brought into harmony by a single intention.

[CHAPTER THREE: THE ISSUE OF THE SUBSTANCES]

17. Another instance is the issue of the substances: that the ones most prior for Aristotle are not those most prior for Plato. Hence, most of those who look into their books judge that there is a difference with respect to the two opinions of both of them concerning this subject. What drew them to this judgment and presumption is their finding in

15. Literally, "his cognized letter" (*risālatuh al-maʿrūfa*).

16. Literally, "their sons" (*banūhā*).

17. Something very much like this is to be found in Abū al-Wafā' al-Mubashshir Ibn al-Fātik, *Mukhtār al-Ḥikam wa Maḥāsin al-Kalim* (Anthology of wise maxims and attractive words), 2d ed., ed. ʿAbd al-Raḥmān Badawī (Beirut: al-Mu'assasa al-ʿArabiyya li-al-Dirāsāt wa al-Nashr, 1980), 184:5-18:

> Plato rebuked him for the wisdom he had made apparent and the books he had compiled; and he answered, excusing himself: Those adept in wisdom and their heirs ought not to sully it; its enemies and those who abstain from it will not obtain it because of their ignorance of what is in it, and their loathing for it and aversion to it will make it difficult for them. I have well fortified this wisdom—in spite of my having divulged it—making it inaccessible so that no fools will climb to it, no ignoramuses obtain it, or scoundrels reach it. And I have given it an organization that will neither trouble the wise nor be of any use to deceitful unbelievers.

See also F. Rosenthal, "Al-Mubashshir ibn Fātik," *Oriens* 13–14 (1960–61): 132–58, for a description of al-Mubashshir's text and its manuscripts intended as a complement to Badawī's edition; and A. J. Arberry, "Plato's Testament to Aristotle," *Bulletin of the School of African Studies* 34 (1971): 475–90.

Plato's statements in many of his books, like the *Timaeus*[18] and the *Young Statesman*,[19] an indication that the most excellent, most prior, and most venerable substance is the one close to the intellect and the soul and far from sense-perception and natural existence. Then they found that in many of Aristotle's statements in his books—such as the book on the *Categories*[20] and his book on *Conditional Syllogisms*[21]—he states explicitly that the substances most worthy of being deemed excellent and prior are the primary substances, namely, individuals. So when they find the dissimilarity and the divergence we have mentioned in these statements, they do not doubt that a difference exists between the two beliefs.

18. But this is not the case, because the procedure of sages and philosophers is to differentiate between statements and propositions in the various arts. Thus they speak about one thing in an art according to the requisites of that art, then speak about the very same thing in another art differently than they first spoke about it. This is neither unprecedented nor excessive,[22] since philosophy hinges on arguing "insofar as" and "with respect to." As the saying goes, were "insofar as" and "with respect to" eliminated, sciences and philosophy would cease to exist. Do you not see that the same individual—Socrates, for example—falls under [6a] substance insofar as he is a human being; under quantity insofar as his whole is measured in terms of one of his parts; under quality insofar as he is white, virtuous, or the like;

18. See Plato, *Timaeus* 51d-52a; the passage is part of Timaeus's general account of the cosmos and its coming into being (see 27a–29e *ff*), but is emphatically endorsed by Timaeus as being consonant with his own opinion.

19. There is much confusion about the second word in this title in the various manuscripts, but it is most likely *Kitāb al-Būlīṭī al-Ṣaghīr*, with Alfarabi probably having in mind Plato's *Statesman*; see 286a (the speaker is not Socrates but the Eleatic Stranger, who first appears in the dialogue dramatically preceding this one—namely, the *Sophist*). Although Alfarabi neither uses this title nor refers to the *Statesman* by name at all in his *Philosophy of Plato*, the discussion of the prince and the statesman in section 21 of that work has often been taken as a reference to this dialogue; see Mahdi, trans., *Philosophy of Plato*, sections 21–22, and Mahdi's note 1 to section 21 referring to pp. 21–22 of the Rosenthal and Walzer edition of the Arabic text. See also Majid Fakhry, "Al-Farabi and the Reconciliation of Plato and Aristotle," *Journal of the History of Ideas* 26 (1965): 474, note 27; and D. M. Dunlop, trans. *Al-Fārābī, Fuṣūl al-Madanī: Aphorisms of the Statesman*, (Cambridge: Cambridge University Press, 1961), pp. 17–18.

20. See Aristotle, *Categories*, 5.2a11–18, 2b15–20, and 3a1–4; Alfarabi refers to this book here by the Arabic transliteration of its Greek title, *Qāṭīghūrīyās*.

21. Aristotle is not known to have written any book with the title *Conditional Syllogisms*—(*Fī al-Qiyāsāt al-Sharṭiyya*)—but see *Prior Analytics*, 1.27.43a40-43, for something similar to what Alfarabi says here.

under relation insofar as he is a father; and under posture insofar as he is sitting? It is the same with all other similar [things].

19. When the sage Aristotle sets individual substances down as the substances most worthy of priority and excellence, he does so only in the art of logic and the art of physics.[23] He takes into account there the conditions of the existing things tangential to what is sense-perceptible, from which everything conjectured is derived and by which the universal concept is constituted. And when the sage Plato sets the universals down as the substances most worthy of priority and excellence, he does so only in metaphysics and in his theological statements. He takes into account there the simple, permanent existing things that neither change nor perish.

20. Since there is a variance between the two purposes, a gap between the two intentions, and a difference in the aims of the two, it is correct that the two opinions of these two sages are in accord and that there is no disagreement between them. However, disagreement would have occurred had the two of them expressed, from the same perspective and in relation to the same intention, judgments about the substances that disagreed. Since this is not the case, it is correct that the two opinions of both of them regarding the priority and excellence of the substances are in harmony about the same issue.

[CHAPTER FOUR: DIVISION AND SYNTHESIS]

21. Another instance, also, is what is presumed about them as concerns the issue of division and synthesis for adequate definitions. It is that Plato is of the opinion adequate definitions can be achieved only by the method of division, while Aristotle maintains [6b] they can be achieved only by the method of demonstration and synthesis.

22. It ought to be known that this is similar to a flight of stairs that one climbs up and another comes down; the distance is the same, although

22. Reading *mustakthar*, with the Diyarbekir manuscript, instead of *mustankar* ("reprehensible"), with the other manuscripts.

23. The text reads *ṣināʿat al-kiyān*. The medieval Islamic philosophers used *kiyān*, which—like *ṭabʿ* and *ṭabīʿa*—means nature, as a way of referring to Aristotle's *Physics*; see A.-M. Goichon, *Lexique de la langue philosophique d'Ibn Sina*, (Paris: Desclée de Brouwer, 1938), p. 357. In section 17, the term *al-wujūd al-kiyānī* occurred and was translated as "natural existence."

there is a difference between the two pursuits. Now Aristotle was of the opinion that the closest and most masterful method for [arriving at] adequate definitions is to seek what characterizes the thing particularly and generally in its essence and substance. This holds also for the rest of what he mentions in the section of his *Metaphysics* where he discusses adequate definitions, as well as in the *Posterior Analytics* and in the treatise in the *Topics* about the topics of definition, which is too long for this statement of ours.[24] Most of his discussions are not without some division, although it may not be explicitly stated. For when he differentiates between the general and the particular or between the essential and the non-essential, he is pursuing the method of division in his nature, his mind, and his thought, while making only some of its terms explicit. For this reason, he does not reject the method of division right away, but counts it as an auxiliary in extracting the parts of the definitions. A sign of this is his statement in the *Prior Analytics* toward the end of the first treatise: "It is easy to recognize that division into genera is a small part of this undertaking," and the rest of what follows that.[25]

Nor does he repeat the meanings that Plato is of an opinion to use when he is intent upon the most general thing he can find that contains what he intends to define. Thus he divides it into two essential differentiae, then divides each of its divisions in the same manner and looks into which of the two domains the thing he intends to define occurs. He then continues doing that until [7a] he obtains something general approximating what he intends to define and a differentia that constitutes its essence and marks it off from what is common to it. He has not thereby escaped a sort of synthesis insofar as he synthesizes the differentia with the genus, even though he was not intent upon this at the outset.

24. Here and in what follows, when referring to sections of Aristotle's *Metaphysics*, Alfarabi says something like "the letter among the letters of the *Metaphysics*," *(al-ḥarf . . . min ḥurūf fī Mā Baʿd al-Ṭabīʿa)*. This unusual formulation points to the traditional designation of the books of the *Metaphysics* in Greek by letters of the alphabet, rather than by numbers; see *Averroès: Tafsīr Mā Baʿd Aṭ-Ṭabīʿat*, ed. Maurice Bouyges (Beirut: Imprimerie Catholique, 1952), pp. cxxiv-cxxv. Similarly, Alfarabi here calls the *Posterior Analytics* the "Book on Demonstration" (*Kitāb al-Burhān*) and the *Topics* the "Book on Dialectic" (*Kitāb al-Jadal*). For the references, see Aristotle, *Metaphysics*, 7.5.1030b14-1031a14 and 7.12.1037b8-1038a35; also 8.6.1045a8-1045b29; *Posterior Analytics*, 2.13.96a20-97b40; and *Topics*, 1.5.101b37-102a17, 1.8.103b12-19, and 1.15.107a36-107b13.

25. See *Prior Analytics*, 1.31.46a31. Note that in "the rest of what follows that," that is, in the rest of the sentence, Aristotle says:"for division is like a weak syllogism, since it begs the point it is to prove and always arrives at a conclusion more general than needed."

23. Since the latter [sc., Aristotle] inevitably uses what the former [sc., Plato] does—although his apparent pursuit is different from the apparent pursuit of the former—and since the former inevitably uses what the latter does—although his apparent pursuit is different from the apparent pursuit of the latter—the meanings are therefore identical. Moreover, it is all the same whether you seek a thing's genus and differentia or seek the thing in its genus and differentia. It is thus apparent that there is no fundamental difference between the two opinions, although there is a difference in the two pursuits. Now we do not claim that there is no gap in any mode or any respect whatever between the two methods, because in that case we would have to maintain that Aristotle's speech, undertaking, and pursuit are exactly the same as Plato's speech, undertaking, and pursuit; and this is absurd and repugnant. We do claim, however, that there is no difference between them about fundamentals and intentions, as we have explained and will [further] explain, God, may He be exalted, willing!

[CHAPTER FIVE: THE SYLLOGISM]

24. Another instance, too, is what has been unduly assumed by Ammonius[26] and many of the schoolmen among those who succeeded him in his movement, the latest of whom is Themistius,[27] to the effect that the conclusion of a mixed necessary and contingent syllogism will be contingent

26. Though the reference here and in section 58 best fits the Ammonius, son of Hermias, who was the head of the school of Alexandria at the end of the fifth century C.E. and beginning of the sixth, Alfarabi's attempt to link Ammonius with Themistius makes it appear that he is referring instead to Ammonius Saccas, ca. 175–250 C.E. The latter was the teacher of Plotinus, contemporary of Origen, and reputed founder of Neoplatonism, whereas the former was a student of Proclus and teacher of Philoponus, Asclepius, Olympiodorus, Damascius, Simplicius, and most likely also of Boethius. Above all, he was responsible for bringing Aristotle's teaching into harmony with Christian doctrine. See Muhsin Mahdi, "Alfarabi against Philoponus," *Journal of Near Eastern Studies* 26 (Oct. 1967) no 4: 233–35 and "The Arabic Text of Alfarabi's 'Against John the Grammarian' " in *Medieval and Middle Eastern Studies in Honor of Aziz Suryal Atiya*, ed. Sami A. Hanna (Leiden: E. J. Brill, 1972), p. 269; also *Dictionnaire des philosophes antiques*, article 140, "Ammonios Saccas," by Richard Goulet, vol. 1, pp. 166–68; and article 141, "Ammonios d'Alexandrie," by Henri Dominique Saffrey and Jean-Pierre Mahé, vol. 1, pp. 168–70.

The term translated in what follows immediately as "movement" is the same one translated heretofore as "procedure" (*madhhab*).

27. Themistius, died 334 C.E., was a Greek philosopher and teacher who gained fame as the author of paraphrases of a number of Aristotle's works.

and not necessary when the major premise is necessary. They attribute that to Plato and claim that in his books he sets forth syllogisms whose major premises are found to be necessary and whose conclusions are contingent. Such is the syllogism he sets forth in the [7b] *Timaeus*, where he says: "Existence is more excellent than non-existence, and nature always longs for what is more excellent."[28] They allege that the conclusion resulting from these two premises, namely, "nature longs for existence," is not necessary in a [number of] respects. One is that there is no necessity in nature and that what is in nature is probable existence. The other is that nature may long for non-existence when existence is consequently accompanied by harm. They allege that the major premise of this syllogism is necessary because of his saying "always." On the other hand, Aristotle explicitly declares that the syllogism whose premises are a mixture of necessary and contingent, with the major being necessary, will accordingly have a necessary conclusion.[29] This is an apparent difference.

25. We say then: There is no statement at all of Plato's in which he explicitly declares that conclusions such as these are either necessary or contingent; that is something only claimed by these later [commentators]. They allege that syllogisms of that approach may be found in Plato, one of them being what we have recounted. What led them to this belief is making few distinctions and mixing up the art of logic with natural science. That is, they find that the syllogism is composed of two premises and three terms—first, middle, and last.[30] And they find that the first term implies the middle in a necessary manner and the middle implies the last in a contingent manner. They are of the opinion that the middle term is itself the cause of the first term implying the last and the connection between the one and the other. And then they find that its state in relation to the last [8a] is contingent. So they say: "If the state of the middle term—which is the cause and reason for the connection of the first with the last—is contingent, how then is it permissible that the state of the first term in relation to the last be necessary?"

What makes this belief tolerable to them is their looking into abstract things and meanings, their turning away from the stipulations of logic

28. Though not precisely the same, an approximation of this syllogism occurs in *Timaeus*, 29e–30a.

29. See *Prior Analytics*, 1.9.30a15–23.

30. See *Prior Analytics*, 1.25.41b36–42b5; also 1.23.40b37–41a13.

and the stipulations of what is said of all,[31] their neglect of the implication resulting for them from what is said of all, and the paucity of their cognition that the pivot of the syllogism is what is said of all. If they knew, took thought about, and reflected upon the state of what is said of all, its stipulation, and its meaning—namely, that if all that is B, all that is included in B, all that becomes B, and all that is described as B is A, and AB exists, then, according to the stipulations of what is said of all, it is A by necessity—no doubt would have occurred to them nor would what they believed have been tolerable to them.[32]

26. Moreover, if the syllogisms they bring forth from Plato are truly reflected upon, most of them will be found[33] to go back to the types[34] of syllogisms composed of two affirmative [premises] in the second figure.[35] And no matter how one looks into each one of these premises, it is evident that what they claim is untenable.

27. Alexander of Aphrodisias[36] has already commented on the meaning of what is said of all and has defended Aristotle in what he claims. In the *Analytics*,[37] we ourselves have also expounded upon his statements deal-

31. See *Prior Analytics*, 1.1.24b28–31; and *Posterior Analytics*, 1.4.73a25–34. The term is *al-maqūl ʿalā al-kull*. For a fuller explanation, see Averroes, *Talkhīṣ Kitāb al-Qiyās*, (Middle Commentary on the *Prior Analytics*), ed. Charles Butterworth et al (Cairo: The General Egyptian Book Organization, 1983), section 8, p. 67.

32. The issue here and in the preceding section is the modality of the premises, an issue Aristotle discusses at great length in the *Prior Analytics*; see 1.2.25a1-22.40b16, esp. 1.9.30a15-23 and 1.12.32a7-14.

33. Reading *yūjad*, with the Princeton Garrett manuscript, rather than *wajadū* ("they would find"), with the majority of the manuscripts.

34. Though all of the manuscripts have *ṣuwar* ("forms"), it is usual to speak of the "types" (*ḍurūb*) of syllogisms in each figure; see sections 29–30.

35. An example would be: "B is predicated of A," and "B is predicated of C." As Aristotle explains, there is no syllogism in this figure when both premises are affirmative; see *Prior Analytics*, 1.5.26b34-28a9, esp. 27b11–12. See also Alfarabi, *Kitāb al-Qiyās*, in *al-Manṭiq ʿind al-Fārābī*, ed. Rafīq al-ʿAjm (Beirut: Dār al-Mashriq, 1986), vol. 2, pp. 25–27, esp. 27:17–18.

36. He was a Peripatetic philosopher and head of the Lyceum between 189 and 211 C.E.

37. Here, Alfarabi speaks simply of the *Anālūṭīqā*. As is evident from the discussion in the preceding section (see note 35), the discussion of this subject is in Book One of the *Prior Analytics*. In his shorter commentary on the *Prior Analytics* referred to in note 35, Alfarabi says nothing about this subject, and only the Second Treatise of his *Long Commentary on Aristotle's Prior Analytics* is extant in Arabic; see Alfarabi, *Sharḥ al-Qiyās* in *al-Manṭiqiyyāt li-al-Fārābī, al-Shurūḥ al-Manṭiqiyya*, vol. 2, ed. Muḥammad Taqī Dānish Pajūh (Qumm: Maktabat Ayyat Allāh al-ʿUẓmā al-Marʿashī al-Najafī, 1409/1989).

ing with this subject, explained the meaning of what is said of all, unequivocally commented on it, and differentiated between the syllogistic and demonstrative necessary in such a manner that anyone who reflects upon it will be spared from whatever occasions bewilderment about this subject.

28. It has, therefore, become apparent that what Aristotle claims about this [8b] syllogism is as he claims and that no statement of Plato is to be found in which he explicitly contradicts Aristotle's statement.

[CHAPTER SIX: SIMILAR CLAIMS]

29. Similarly, they [sc., the commentators] claim that Plato uses the type of syllogism in the first and third figures whose minor premise is negative. Aristotle has already explained this in the Prior *Analytics*,[38] showing that it is not conclusive.

30. Moreover, the ancient commentators have already discussed this doubt, analyzed it, and explained it. We ourselves have also expounded upon it in our long commentaries and have explained that what Plato sets forth in the *Republic*[39] and likewise Aristotle in his *On the Heavens*[40] leads one to conjecture that they are negations, but in fact they are not. Rather, they are retractive affirmations, as in his saying "the heaven is not-light and not-heavy." And it is the like with whatever is similar, since subjects with respect to them do exist. Whenever retractive affirmations occur in the syllogism, it is not impossible for the syllogism to be conclusive—whereas if they were to occur as simple negations, they would lead to [syllogistic] types that are not conclusive.

38. Here, Alfarabi speaks of Aristotle's *Prior Analytics* by its more formal title, *Anālūṭīqā al-Ūlā*. For the reference, see *Prior Analytics*, 1.4.26a2-8 and 1.6.28a38-28b4.

39. Literally, "Book of the Regime" (*Kitāb al-Siyāsa*). Except for his use of the term *Ablīṭīyā*—see sections 57 and 64—this is the way Alfarabi refers to the *Republic* in the rest of the treatise.

40. The work is referred to here by its usual Arabic title, *On the Heaven and the World* (*Fī al-Samā' wa al-ʿĀlam*). Even though the Greek title of Aristotle's book is simply *On the Heavens* (*Peri Ouranou*), it is given this longer title in Arabic. For the reference, see Aristotle, *On the Heavens*, 1.3.269b30. An explanation in keeping with what Alfarabi says here occurs in Averroes, *Talkhīṣ. al-Samā' wa al-ʿĀlam* (Middle commentary on *On the Heaven and the World*), ed. Jamāl al-Dīn al-ʿAlawī (Fez: Kulliyyat al-Adāb, 1984), pp. 83–84.

[CHAPTER SEVEN: ADDITIONAL CLAIMS]

31. Another instance, also, is what Aristotle sets forth in Chapter Five of *On Interpretation*,[41] namely, that the negation of an affirmation having one of the contraries as a predicate is more contrary than the affirmation whose predicate is the contrary of that predicate. Now many people presume that Plato differs with him about this opinion and is himself of the opinion that the affirmation whose predicate is contrary to the predicate of the other affirmation is more contrary. They prove that [9a] by many of his political and ethical statements, such as his mentioning in the *Republic*: "There is no justice intermediate between justice and injustice."[42]

32. However, what Aristotle is aiming at in *On Interpretation* and what Plato is aiming at in the *Republic* have eluded these [people], because the two intended purposes are divergent. Aristotle is only explaining the [logical] opposition of statements and looking into which of them exhibits the more intense and the more general opposition. A sign of this is in the proofs he adduces and his explaining that some things admit of no contrariety whatever, even though there is nothing that does not have negatives opposed to it:

> Moreover, even if this must be the case in what we have not mentioned, we are still of the opinion that what has been said about this is correct. That is, either the contradictory belief must be the contrary in every case or not a contrary in any case at all. However, with things that admit of no contrary at all, falsehood is the belief opposing the truth. For exam-

41. The work is referred to here by something approaching an Arabic transliteration of its Greek title; that is, the Greek *Peri Hermēneias* is rendered as *Bārīrmanīyās* (or, perhaps, *Bāryirmanīyās*, or even *Bārīrmanyās*). What Alfarabi here calls Chapter Five actually corresponds to Chapter Fourteen of Aristotle's *On Interpretation*; see 23b15–40 and also 17b7–22. See also *Sharḥ al-Fārābī li-Kitāb Arisṭūṭālīs fī al-ʿIbāra* (Alfarabi's long commentary on Aristotle's *De Interpretatione*), ed. Wilhelm Kutsch and Stanley Marrow (Beirut: Imprimérie Catholique, 1960), 206:23-211:24 and 67:3–71: 12. F. W. Zimmermann has translated this work into English, giving indications of the pages and lines of the Kutsch-Marrow edition in the margins of his translation; see *Al-Farabi's Commentary and Short Treatise on Aristotle's De Interpretatione* (London: Oxford University Press, 1981), pp. 200–211 and 60–66.

42. See Plato, *Republic*, 2.359a. In order to goad Socrates into saying what justice is, Glaucon explains what people claim to be the origin of justice: for them, it is the mean between doing injustice without being punished and suffering injustice without having revenge. Socrates' final answer to Glaucon's challenge is set forth at 9.588b–592b.

ple, he who presumes that a human being is not a human being has actually made a false presumption. Even though these two beliefs are contraries, in all other beliefs the contrary is nothing but the contradictory belief.[43]

33. Now when Plato explained that there is no justice intermediate between justice and injustice, he only intended to explain political ideas and their ranks, not the opposition of arguments within them. And Aristotle has mentioned in his "Book to Young Nicomachus about Politics" something similar to what Plato has explained.[44]

34. Hence it should be clear to anyone who considers those statements [9b] and looks into them equitably that there is no difference between the two opinions and no divergence between the two beliefs. On the whole, no statements by Plato have yet been found in which he expounds the log-

43. This passage is a literal citation of Isḥāq Ibn Ḥunayn's translation of Aristotle's *De Interpretatione* 14.23b27-32; see *Kitāb al-ʿIbāra* in *Manṭiq Arisṭū*, ed. ʿAbd al-Raḥmān Badawī (Cairo: Maṭbaʿa Dār al-Kutub al-Miṣriyya, 1948), vol. 1, 97:16–98:4, with minor differences: *yurā* ("he is of the opinion"), instead of *nurā* ("we are of the opinion") in line 2; *aṣlan* ("at all") omitted in line 5; and *wa* ("and") added before *mithāl dhālika* ("for example") in line 7. Alfarabi quotes the first sentence of the passage in his *Long Commentary on Aristotle's De Interpretatione* and comments on it; then, omitting the next sentence, he cites the remainder of the passage and comments on it; see *Sharḥ al-Fārābī li-Kitāb Arisṭūṭālīs fī al-ʿIbāra*, 210:16–17 with 210:18–211:12 and 211:14–18 with 211:19–214:28; also *Al-Farabi's Commentary and Short Treatise on Aristotle's De Interpretatione*, 204–5 and 205–10.

English translations of the Greek passage vary slightly from the English translation of Isḥāq Ibn Ḥunayn's Arabic version that appears here. In J. L. Ackrill's translation of Aristotle's text, for example, we find:

> Further, if in other cases also the same must hold, it would seem that we have given the correct account of this one as well. For either everywhere that of the contradiction is the contrary, or nowhere. But in cases where there *are* no contraries there is still a false belief, the one opposite to the true one; e.g. he who thinks that the man is not a man is deceived. If, therefore, these are contraries, so too elsewhere are the beliefs of the contradiction.

See *Aristotle's Categories and De Interpretatione*, trans. J. L. Ackrill (Oxford: Clarendon Press, 1963), pp. 66–67 (the emphasis is Ackrill's).

44. Although the language is admittedly strange (*Kitābuh ilā Nīqūmākhus al-Ṣaghīr fī al-Siyāsa*), this seems to be a reference to Aristotle's *Nicomachean Ethics*; see Book 5, Chapters 1–9, esp. 3.1131b16-17, 4.1132b18-19, 9.1136b15-29, and 9.1137a27-30. In the introduction to his edition of Isḥāq Ibn Ḥunayn's translation of Aristotle's *Nicomachean Ethics*, ʿAbd al-Raḥmān Badawī defers to Ṣāʿid al-Andalusī's claim that this *Nīqūmākhus al-Ṣaghīr* work is distinct from either the *Nicomachean Ethics* or the *Eudemian Ethics*; see *al-Akhlāq, Taʾlīf Arisṭūṭālīs, Tarjamat Isḥāq Ibn Ḥunayn*, ed. ʿAbd al-Raḥmān Badawī (Kuwait: Wikālat al-Maṭbūʿāt, 1979), pp. 22–25. Yet see section 44 and note 59.

ical ideas so many people allege that he and Aristotle differ about. Rather they prove what they allege by means of his various political, ethical, and theological statements—as we have already mentioned.

[CHAPTER EIGHT: THE CONDITION OF VISION]

35. Another instance, also, is the condition of vision and its manner; Plato is attributed with having an opinion about it that differs from Aristotle's. Aristotle is of the opinion that vision comes about as an affection of the eye,[45] whereas Plato is of the opinion that vision occurs from something emanating from the eye and encountering the object of vision. Commentators from both camps have gone into excess in dealing with this question, adducing proofs, repugnant things, and forced meanings. They have twisted the statements of the leaders away from their intended customary usages,[46] given them interpretations that facilitate repugnant things, and evaded the method of truth and fairness.

36. When Aristotle's disciples heard Plato's disciples say that vision comes about by something emanating from the eye, they said: Now emanation pertains only to a body, and this body that they allege emanates from the eye is either air, light, or fire. If it is air, air already exists in what is between the eye and the object of vision; what need is there, then, for the emanation of additional air?

If it is light, light also already exists in the air that is between the eye and the object of vision; so the emanation of another light is superfluous and not needed. Moreover, if it is light, why does it simultaneously need [10a] motionless light between the eye and the object of vision? Why is this light that emanates from the eye not able to dispense with the light that it needs in the air? And why does one not see in the dark if what emanates from the eye is light? Moreover, if it is said that the light emanating from the eye is weak, why then does it not become more powerful when many eyes converge to look at the same thing at night, as light is seen to become more powerful with the convergence of many lamps?

45. Literally, "sight" (*al-baṣar*). In this whole discussion, *baṣar*—rather than the more usual *'ayn*—is used to denote eye. For Aristotle's views, see *On the Soul*, 2.7.418a27–419a25; and for Plato's views, see *Timaeus*, 45b–46a and 67c–68d.

46. The term is *sunan*, the plural of *sunna*.

If it is fire, why does it not get hot and burn as fire does? Why is it not extinguished in water as fire is extinguished? Why does it penetrate downward as it penetrates upward, when fire is not such as to penetrate downward?[47]

Again, if it is said that what emanates from the eye is something other than these aforementioned things, why is there not clashing and colliding at the point of intersection of things looked at[48] so that those who are looking while facing one another are prevented from visual perception? These and similar repugnant things became tolerable to them when they distorted the utterance "emanation" from its popular intent and stretched it to the emanation that is said of bodies.[49]

37. Then, when Plato's disciples heard Aristotle's disciples saying that vision comes about from an affection, they distorted this utterance and said: Affection is inevitably either being influenced, transformed, or qualitatively changed. This affection takes place either in the organ of vision or in the transparent body that is between the eye[50] and the object of vision. If it takes place in the organ of vision, it follows that the pupil is transformed in a single instant from an infinite number of colors into an infinite number [10b] of colors, which is absurd. For transformation occurs without fail over time and from one specific thing to another, definite thing. And if it is said that the part of the pupil that perceives white is other than the part that perceives black, it follows that these parts are separate and distinct, but they are not. If that affection attaches to the transparent body—that is, the air that is between the eye and the object of vision—it follows that a single subject admits of two contraries at the same moment, which is absurd. These and similar [arguments] are some of the repugnant things they have adduced.

38. Then Aristotle's disciples presented proofs for the soundness of what they claimed and said: If it were not that colors and their substitutes were actually carried by the transparent body, the eye would not perceive the stars and very distant objects instantaneously. Indeed, what is transferred

47. See *On the Heavens*, 1.2.269a18-19.

48. Here and in the rest of the sentence, Alfarabi changes from the verb *baṣara* and its derivatives to the verb *naẓara* and its derivatives.

49. For the objections set forth here, see Aristotle, *On Sense and Sensible Objects*, 2.437a19-439a3, esp. 437a27-438b16.

50. See note 45.

undoubtedly reaches the proximate distance before reaching the remote one. Yet, despite the remoteness of the distance, we observe the stars at the same moment that we observe what is closer; and there is no delay in that. Hence, it appears from this that the air that is actually transparent carries the colors of the objects of vision and conveys [them] to the eye.

39. Plato's disciples presented proofs for the soundness of their claim that something issues and emanates from the eye and encounters the object of vision by [saying] that when the objects of vision are at varying distances, our perception of what is closer to the eye is more complete and more perfect than our perception of what is more distant. The cause of this is that the thing emanating from the eye perceives by its power what is closer to it; [11a] it then continues to weaken, and its perception diminishes bit by bit until its power wanes and it does not at all perceive what is very remote from it. What confirms this claim is that whenever we extend our sight across a great distance and fix it on an object silhouetted by the light of a nearby fire, we perceive that object even if the distance between it and us is dark. If the matter were as Aristotle's disciples say, it would be necessary for the entire distance between us and the object of vision to be illuminated in order to carry the color and convey [it] to the eye. But since we find that the silhouetted body is visible from a distance, we know that something emanates from the eye, extends and cuts through the darkness, reaches the object of vision silhouetted by a certain light, and then perceives it.

40. If both camps would let their eyes relax a little, moderate their glance, aim at the truth, and abandon the way of prejudice, they would know that the meaning the Platonists wanted by the utterance "emanation"[51] is other than the meaning of a body going out from one place [to another]. What compels them to articulate the utterance "emanation" is the constraint of expression, the narrowness of the language, and the lack of an utterance that denotes the issuing of [natural] powers without giving the image of a "going out" that pertains to bodies. And [they would know] also that the meaning Aristotle's disciples intended by the utterance "affection" is other than the meaning of affection which is in quality along with transformation and change.[52] It is apparent that what is com-

51. Here and throughout this discussion, the term is *khurūj* and means "going out."

52. For Aristotle's explanations of affection that is in quality, see *Categories*, 8.9a28-10a10, esp. 9a36-9b1, and also *Metaphysics*, 5.21.1022b15-21.

pared to a certain thing is other than that to which it is compared in its essence and substance.[53]

When we look into this matter equitably, we know that there is a power here linking the eye to the visible object; visual perception takes place by means of it in a manner [11b] other than that by which a body is linked with another body. And [we also know] that he who terms repugnant the argument of Plato's disciples that a certain power emanates from the eye and encounters the object of vision has an argument no less repugnant than theirs when he says that the air carries the color of the object of vision and then conveys it to the eye so that it physically encounters it. Everything that follows from the statements of the former about the issuing and emanation of a power follows as well from the statement of the latter concerning the air carrying colors and conveying them to the eyes.

41. It is apparent that these and similar things are subtle and fine notions that are accorded special attention and investigated by those who pretend to be philosophers. They were forced to express themselves in utterances close to these notions, for they found no simple utterances [already] set down to express the truth of the matter without equivocation. This being the case, detractors have found an opportunity to argue; and so they have. Most of the controversy about notions like these occurs for the reasons we have mentioned. That is inevitably due to one of two things: the backwardness of the opponent or his willfulness. But he who is possessed of a sound mind, solid opinion, and upright intellect—if he is not determined upon falsification, prejudice, or contention—will seldom hold a belief different from [that of] a learned human being who,

53. The term is *inniyya*. For this understanding of the term, see Alfarabi, *Kitāb al-Alfāẓ al-Mustaʿmala fī al-Manṭiq* (The book of utterances employed in logic), ed. Muhsin Mahdi (Beirut: Dār al-Mashriq, 1968), 45:4–10:

> There are particles that are joined to something to signify that the thing's existence is established and its correctness firm, like our saying *inna* with a *shadda* on the *nūn*. For example, there is our saying "*inna* God is one" and "*inna* the world is finite." Therefore, the existence of something is sometimes called its *inniyya*, and the essence of a thing is called its *inniyya*. Likewise, the substance of something is also called its *inniya*. Thus we frequently use our saying "the *inniya* of something" instead of our saying "the substance of something". For we are of the opinion that there is no difference between our saying, "What is the substance of this garment?" and saying, "What is its *inniya*?" Yet the latter is not as generally known as the former among the multitude; and the practitioners of the sciences use the latter frequently.

when seeking to explain an obscure matter and elucidate a subtle notion, necessarily articulates an utterance that does not relieve the one forming a concept of it of the confusion befalling equivocal and metaphorical utterances.[54]

[CHAPTER NINE: MORAL HABITS OF THE SOUL]

42. Another instance is the moral habits of the soul and their presuming that Aristotle's opinion about them differs from Plato's opinion. That is because Aristotle explicitly declares in his *Nicomachean Ethics*[55] that [12a] all moral habits are habits, that they undergo change, that none of them is by nature, and that a human being is capable of moving from one to another by habituation. Plato explicitly declares in the *Republic* and especially in the *Statesman* that nature prevails over habit; that whenever the mature become naturally inclined to a certain moral habit, it is difficult for them to break it; and that when they do intend to break that moral habit, they become more embedded in it.[56] To illustrate this, he cites the example of a tree that has intruded upon a road by its inclination and crookedness: If one intends to clear the road, it must be pulled in the other direction; otherwise, if we leave it to its course, it will take more from the road than it already has.[57] No one who hears these two discourses will doubt that there is a difference between Aristotle and Plato on the issue of moral habits.

43. In truth, the matter is not as they presume because in his book known as the *Nicomachea* Aristotle discusses the political laws, as we have

54. In other words, such a person will discern what this learned person is trying to explain and will do so despite the ambiguities of the explanation.

55. Literally, "The Book of Nicomachea" (*Kitāb Nīqūmākhīyā*); see note 44. For the reference here, see *Nicomachean Ethics*, 2.1.1103a15-1103b2; see also *Categories*, 8.8b27–9a13.

56. In the *Republic*, especially at 7.518d-e, Socrates seems to agree that ordinary virtues can be produced by habituation. The capacity for other virtues, however, like the aptitude for wisdom, must be innate or natural and thus cannot be produced by habituation alone; see 518e–519a. In the *Statesman*, at 308e–309a, the Eleatic Stranger states that there are some who do not have the capacity to acquire any virtues because they have a defective or evil nature.

57. There is no passage in either of these works that sets forth such an example. In the *Republic*, however, Socrates does discuss plants and the way their cultivation resembles the education of children in moral habits; see 6.491d–492b. See also Richard Walzer, "New Light on Galen's Moral Philosophy," in *Greek into Arabic: Essays on Islamic Philosophy*, (Cambridge: Harvard University Press, 1962), pp. 158–59; and Aristotle, *Nicomachean Ethics*, 2.9.1109b5-7.

already explained in a number of places in our commentary on that book.[58] Even had he also discussed moral habits, as Porphyry and many later commentators say [he did], his discussion would have been about moral laws—and a legal discussion is always universal and unconditional, and not relative to anything else. Clearly, if looked at unconditionally, each moral habit will be known to be subject to being transformed and altered, albeit with difficulty and strain; nor is anything pertaining to the moral habits exempt from change and transformation.

An infant whose soul is still potential does not actually possess any of the moral habits, sciences, or traits [12b] in general; he possesses them only potentially. And as long as he is in potentiality, he has the capacity to receive a thing or its contrary. Whenever he acquires one of two contraries, it is possible to break him of the acquired contrary by the other, unless his constitution weakens and he is afflicted by a kind of decay—like what occurs to one subject to privation and abundance who becomes such that the two [contraries] no longer alternately obtain in him due to a kind of decay and lack of capacity. If this is so, then no moral habit—if looked into unconditionally—is by nature exempt from change and alteration.

44. Plato looks into the kinds of political regimes—which are easier and which more difficult [to establish], which more useful and which more harmful. He looks into the conditions of those who bring about and those who found regimes—which of them do so more easily and which with more difficulty. Upon my life, anyone reared in a certain moral habit will have great difficulty breaking it; but what is difficult is not impossible. Aristotle does not deny that for some people and some individuals it is easier to transfer from one moral habit to another and for others it is

58. There are many references in the ancient bibliographers to this commentary by Alfarabi on the Nicomachean Ethics, but it has not come down to us. In his *Ta'rīkh al-Ḥukamā'* (History of the sages), al-Qifṭī includes a *Kitāb al-Akhlāq* (Book of moral habits) among Alfarabi's works; see J. Lippert, ed. (Leipzig: Dieterich'sche Verlagsbuchhandlung, 1903), p. 279. Ibn Abī Usaybiʿa mentions a commentary (*sharḥ*) on the beginning of the book on ethics by Aristotle; see *ʿUyūn al-Anbā' fī Ṭabaqāt al-Aṭibbā'* (Sources of information about the classes of physicians), ed. A. Müller (Königsberg: 1884), vol. 2, p. 138. Finally, in his *Kitāb al-Fihrist* (Catalogue), (Cairo: Maṭbaʿat al-Istiqāma, n.d.), p. 382, Ibn al-Nadīm lists a commentary on a piece (*qiṭʿa*) from Alfarabi's book on ethics by Aristotle. Yet in his summary of Aristotle's philosophy, the *Philosophy of Aristotle*, Alfarabi says nothing about having commented on the *Nicomachean Ethics*.

The term used for "laws" here and in the next sentence is *al-qawānīn*, literally, "canons"; similarly, a derivative, *al-qānūnī*, is translated as "legal" rather than "canonic." In his political treatises, Alfarabi rarely has occasion to use either one.

harder, as he has explicitly declared in his book known as *Nicomachea Minor*.[59] He enumerated the reasons for the difficulty and ease of transferring from one moral habit to another—how many they are, what they are, how each one of these reasons [functions], and what facilitates or impedes them.

45. Whoever reflects on these statements truly and gives everything in them its due will recognize that there is no difference between the two [sages] in truth. This is something the surface [meaning] of the statements makes one imagine when one looks into each statement separately without considering the context [13a] of the particular statement, its rank, and the science to which it belongs.

46. Here is a fundamental of great usefulness for the conceptualization of the sciences, especially in situations like these: namely,[60] that just as whenever matter is conceived of as having a certain form and another form then arises in it, it becomes—along with its [original] form—matter for the form arising in it. Then, if a third form arises in it, it becomes, along with both its [earlier] forms, matter for the third form arising in it. This is like wood, which has a form making it diverge from all other bodies. Then planks are made out of it, and then a bed is made out of the planks. Thus the form of the bed arises in the planks, and the planks are matter for it. And in the planks, which are matter in relation to the form of the bed, are many other forms—like the plank-form, the wood-form, the plant-form,[61] and other eternal forms. So, too, whenever the soul is shaped by a given moral habit and then undertakes to acquire a new moral habit, the moral habits it already has are like things natural to it while the newly-acquired ones are habitual. Then, if it continues in this way, persists, and undertakes to acquire a third moral habit, those [previously acquired ones] will take on the position of the natural in relation to this newly-acquired one.

So whenever you see Plato or anyone else saying that some moral habits are natural and others acquired, know what we have mentioned concerning this and understand the tenor of their statements, lest you find

59. See note 44. Perhaps Alfarabi is referring here to the *Eudemian Ethics*; see 3.2.2.1230a37-1230b21. See also *Nicomachean Ethics*, 3.12.1119a22-1119b18.

60. This is the beginning of a long comparison that takes the form of a single sentence in the Arabic. The significant comparison is between matter and the soul, and the part pertaining to the soul begins with the words "so, too, whenever the soul."

61. The point is that the plant gives rise to a tree, from which wood is fashioned.

the matter problematic and presume that some moral habits are truly impossible to break. For that is very repugnant, and the utterance itself is self-contradictory if you reflect upon it.

[CHAPTER TEN: ABOUT LEARNING AND RECOLLECTION]

47. [13b] Another instance, too, is what Plato expounds in his book known as the *Phaedo*: that learning is recollection.[62] He illustrates that by proofs he recounts from the questioning and answering Socrates had with Simmias on the subject of the equal and equality. That is, equality exists in the soul, and when a human being senses the equal—like a piece of wood or anything else equal to something else—he recollects the equality that is in his soul and thus knows that this equal is equal only due to an equality similar to that existing in the soul. And likewise the rest of what he learns is only his recollecting what is in the soul.

Similarly, in his book known as the *Meno*, he expresses the doubt Aristotle recounts in the *Posterior Analytics* about anyone seeking knowledge inevitably doing so in one of two ways: he is seeking either what he is ignorant of or what he knows.[63] If he is seeking what he is ignorant of, how will he be certain that his knowledge, when he does come to know, is what he is seeking? And if he already knows it, his quest for additional knowledge is superfluous and unnecessary. Then he draws out the discussion in that book to [urge] that he who seeks knowledge of a certain thing seeks in something else only what already definitely exists in his soul—like the equality and inequality existing in the soul. Someone who, for example, seeks to know whether a piece of wood is equal or unequal [to something else] seeks only which of the two it definitely is. When he finds one of them, it is as though he has recollected what was existing in the soul. He thus associates the piece of wood and its condition with what was with him previously: if it was equal, then with equality; if it was unequal, then with [14a] inequality.[64]

62. See *Phaedo*, 72e–76c; also *Meno*, 81c–86c.

63. See *Posterior Analytics*, 1.1.71a1-71b8, esp. 71a29; and Plato, *Meno*, 80d-e. Note, however, that the doubt as formulated here by Alfarabi is Socrates' restatement of Meno's position. Aristotle raises the question of the *Meno* to show why "all rational teaching and learning come from what is previously cognized" (71a1-2) and claims the aporia of the *Meno* to be that "one can learn nothing or only what has been seen" (71a30).

64. See *Phaedo*, 72e–76c; *Meno*, 81d-86c; also *Posterior Analytics*, 2.19.99b15–34 and 100a3-100b17.

48. Most people have made presumptions regarding these arguments that go beyond all limits. Those inclined to the argument about the soul's remaining after it separates from the body go to extremes in interpreting these arguments, distort them from their customary usages,[65] and blithely presume to treat them as demonstrations. They do not know that Plato is merely recounting them on Socrates' authority in the manner of someone who wishes to verify a concealed matter by means of signs and allusions. But a syllogism based on signs is not a demonstration, as the sage Aristotle has made known to us in the *Prior* and *Posterior Analytics*.[66]

Those who deny it [sc., the perdurance of the soul] have also gone to extremes in being repugnant and claimed that Aristotle differs from him [sc., Plato] regarding this opinion. They overlook his statement at the beginning of the *Posterior Analytics* where he begins by saying: "All instruction and all learning proceed only from previously existing cognition." Then, shortly thereafter, he says: "A human being may learn some things of which he had previous knowledge; other things he knows insofar as he learns about them at the same time—for example, all of the existing things that fall under the universals."[67]

Oh, I wish I knew how the meaning of this statement departs in any way from what Plato says! However, an upright intellect, solid opinion, and an inclination to truth and fairness are wanting in most people. Hence, he who thoroughly and salutarily reflects upon the way knowledge, first premises, and learning are obtained will know that no divergence or difference exists between the opinions of the two sages on this point. We are pointing out a slight part of it, just enough to make the meaning clear so as to dissipate [14b] the doubts regarding it.

49. Thus we say: it is manifestly clear that an infant possesses a soul that knows potentially and that has senses as instruments of perception. Sensory perception is only of particulars, and universals are obtained from particulars. Universals are experiences in truth. However, some experiences are obtained intentionally, others unintentionally.[68] It is customary

65. See note 46.

66. Here, Alfarabi refers to these writings by their traditional title, *Anālūṭīqā al-Ūlā wa al-Thāniyya*. The reference to the *Posterior Analytics* in the sentence after the next is, however, to the "Book on Demonstration" (*Kitāb al-Burhān*). For the teaching in question here, see *Prior Analytics*, 2.27.70a3–70b38, esp. 70a3–10; and *Posterior Analytics*, 1.6.74b5–75a37.

67. See *Posterior Analytics*, 1.2.71a17–19; also 71a19–29.

for the multitude to call the universals obtained from a prior intention "experiences." Those a human being obtains unintentionally either have no name among the multitude, because they are not concerned about them, or have a name among the learned: thus they call them "first things," "cognitions," "principles of demonstration," and similar names.

50. In the *Posterior Analytics*, Aristotle has explained that he who loses a certain sense loses a certain knowledge.[69] Indeed, cognitions are obtained in the soul only by means of the senses. When cognitions are obtained in the soul only unintentionally and at the outset, a human being does not recollect when any part of them was obtained. Most people thus conjecture that they have always been in the soul and that there is a way to [obtain] knowledge other than by means of the senses. When such experiences are obtained in the soul, it begins to intellect, since intellect is nothing but experiences. The more of these experiences there are, the more complete an intellect will the soul be.

Moreover, whenever a human being intends to be cognizant of a certain thing and yearns to grasp one of its conditions, he undertakes to associate that thing with its condition by means of what he already knows. That is nothing [15a] but seeking what of that thing is existing in his soul. Thus when he yearns to be cognizant of whether a certain thing is living or not living, and the meaning of living and not living has already been obtained in his soul, he seeks either one of the two meanings by means of his mind, his senses, or both together; once he comes upon it, he becomes calm, feels assured, and delights in being released from the pain of perplexity and ignorance.

51. This is what the sage Plato says, namely, learning is recollection. For learning is but undertaking to know, and recollection undertaking to remember. And the yearning seeker is someone with a certain undertaking. Accordingly, whenever he finds allusions, signs, and meanings of what was previously in his soul in what he intends to cognize, it is as though he recollects it at that point. It is like someone looking at a body some of whose accidental characteristics resemble the accidental characteristics of another body he had been cognizant of but had forgotten; he

68. Here and in what follows, this might also be understood as "spontaneously" (*ghair qaṣad*).

69. See *Posterior Analytics*, 1.18.81a38–39.

then recollects it by what he perceives of its likeness. Intellect, without the senses, has no function peculiar to it except for [seizing] what is similar and conjecturing about the conditions of existing things being otherwise. For the senses perceive the condition of a composite being as composite, that of a separate being as separate, that of a base being as base, that of a noble being as noble, and so forth. Intellect, on the other hand, perceives the condition of each being as the senses perceive it and [perceives] its contrary as well. It thus perceives the condition of a composite being as both composite and separate, the condition of a separate being as both separate and composite, and so forth with the rest of similar things.

52. Hence, whoever reflects upon our brief description of what the sage Aristotle has spoken extensively about at the end of the *Posterior Analytics* [15b] and in the *De Anima*,[70] and that has been expounded upon and closely investigated by the commentators, will know that what the sage mentions at the beginning of the *Posterior Analytics*, and which we have recounted in this argument, is close to what Plato has said in the *Phaedo*. There is, however, a difference between the two positions. That is, the sage Aristotle mentions this when he wants to clarify the question of knowledge[71] and the syllogism, whereas Plato mentions what he mentions when he wants to clarify the issue of the soul. For this reason, it has become problematic for most of those who look into their statements. What we have adduced is sufficient for anyone intent upon the right approach.

[CHAPTER ELEVEN: THE ISSUE OF WHETHER THE WORLD IS ETERNAL OR GENERATED]

53. Another is the issue of the world's being eternal or generated, whether it does or does not have an artisan who is its efficient cause. Some presume that Aristotle is of the opinion that the world is eternal and Plato of a different opinion, that is, that he is of the opinion that the world is generated and has a maker.[72]

70. For the reference to the *Posterior Analytics*, see note 64. For De Anima, see 2.4.417b22–27, 3.3.427a18–427b15, 4.429a10–429b23, and 7.413a1–431b19.

71. Reading *al-ʿilm*, with all of the manuscripts except the Diyarbekir and Princeton Garrett manuscripts, which read *al-ʿālim* ("the one who knows").

72. The term is *fāʿil* from the verb *faʿala* ("to make" or "to do"). When the adjective form occurred in the preceding sentence to modify "cause," it was translated as "efficient" (*ʿillatuh al-fāʿila*).

54. I say: what leads these people to such a base and reprehensible presumption about Aristotle is his saying in the *Topics* that with one and the same proposition it is possible to formulate a syllogism based on widely-held premises for each of its two extremes, for example, whether the world is eternal or not eternal.[73] It has escaped those who disagree that, first, what is set forth as an example does not stand as a belief and, also, that Aristotle's purpose in the *Topics* is not to explain about the world; instead, his purpose is to explain about syllogisms composed of widely-held premises. He had found the people of his time disputing the question of whether the world is eternal [16a] or generated, just as they used to dispute about whether pleasure is good or bad, and supporting each of the two extremes of each question by syllogisms based on widely-held premises. In that book and in his other books, Aristotle explained that the truth and falsehood of a generally accepted premise is not to be taken into account. For what is generally accepted may be false, yet is not discarded in dialectic because of its falseness; or it may be true and is thus used in dialectic because of its being generally accepted, and in demonstration because of its being true. Hence, it is apparent that it is not possible to ascribe to him the belief that the world is eternal due to the example he sets forth in this book.

55. What also leads them to this presumption is what he mentions in the book *On the Heavens* about the whole having no temporal beginning,[74] for they presume that he is there speaking about the world's being eternal. That is not the case, since he had already explained in that and in other books about physics and theology that time is only the number of the motion of the celestial sphere and is generated from it.[75] Now what is generated from a thing does not contain that thing. The meaning of his statement that the world has no temporal beginning is that it did not come into

73. Here and in what follows, Alfarabi refers to the *Topics* by the title *Kitāb Ṭūbīqā* rather than *Kitāb al-Jadal* (Book of dialectic) as he did in section 22. The formulation of what Aristotle says in the *Topics*, 1.11.104b12–18, is somewhat awkward here, but the point becomes clearer in what follows; see also Alfarabi, *Kitāb al-Jadal* in *al-Manṭiq ʿind al-Fārābī*, ed. Rafīq al-ʿAjam (Beirut: Dār al-Mashriq, 1986), vol. 3, 80:7–82:14. Aristotle is merely explaining, as part of his introduction to dialectical reasoning, that there is such confusion with respect to some questions that it is sometimes possible to argue either side of a proposition and to find persuasive premises to support such arguments. See also *Topics*, 1.2.101a25-101b4; and Alfarabi, *Kitāb al-Jadal*, 32:11–34:20.

74. See *On the Heavens*, 1.10.279b17–33.

75. See *On the Heavens*, 1.9.279a15; at 2.4.287a24–27, Aristotle identifies the revolution of the heaven as constituting the measure for motion.

being gradually in parts as plants come into being, for example, or animals. For what comes into being gradually in parts has some parts that precede others in time—time being generated from the motion of the celestial sphere. Thus there cannot possibly be a temporal beginning for its being generated. From that it is valid that it came to be only by the Creator, may His majesty be magnified, innovating it in one stroke and in no time; and from its motion, time is generated.

56. Whoever looks into his statements on Lordship in the book known as the *Theology*[76] [16b] will no longer be confused about his affirming [the existence] of the Artisan, the Innovator of this world. Indeed, in these statements the issue is too manifest to be concealed. There he explains that primary matter has been innovated by the Creator, may He be glorified and magnified, out of nothing, and that it has become corporeal by the Creator, may His majesty be magnified, and by His will, then set in order. He has also explained in the *Physics* and, similarly, in *On the Heavens* that the whole could not be generated by fortune and chance.[77] This can further be inferred from the innovative order that is found among some parts of the world with respect to others.

He has also explained there the issue of the causes—how many they are—and affirmed the efficient cause. And he has also explained there the issue of the bringer into being and the mover and that it is other than the brought into being and the moved.[78] And just as Plato, in his book known as the *Timaeus*, has explained that whatever is brought into being is

76. This book is referred to here and in what follows as *Uthūlūjīyā*, but is more commonly known as *Uthūlūjīyā Arisṭūṭālīs* or *Uthūlūjīyā Arisṭāṭālīs*. It is a pseudo-Aristotelian work that consists of a running paraphrase of the eight sections of the last three books of Plotinus's *Enneads*. The text has been published by ʿAbd al-Raḥmān Badawī in his *Aflūṭīn ʿind al-ʿArab* (Plotinus among the Arabs), (Cairo: Dār al-Nahḍa al-ʿArabiyya, 1966), pp. 3–164. See also *Dictionnaire des philosophes antiques*, article 414, "Aristote de Stagire," especially the section by Maroun Aouad entitled "La *Théologie d'Aristote* et autres textes du *Plotinus* Arabus," vol. 1, pp. 541–90; and Gerhard Endress, *Proclus Arabus: Zwanzig Abschnitte aus der Institutio Theologica in arabischer Übersetzung*, eingeleitet, herausgegeben, und erklärt (Beirut: 1973).

The term translated here as "Lordship" is *al-rubūbiyya*. Though admittedly awkward in English, it is important to distinguish what Alfarabi means by *rubūbiyya* ("Lordship") from what he terms *ilāhiyya* ("divinity") and, immediately below, *rūḥāniyya* ("spirituality"). Moreover, awkward as are "Lordship" and "Lordly" in English, they point to notions more in keeping with theology—which is the point here—than do the terms "sovereignty" and "sovereign."

77. See *Physics*, 2.5.196b10-7.198b3 and *On the Heavens*, 2.8.290a30-35.

78. See *Physics*, 2.3.194b16-7.199b32 and 8.4.254b7-9.266a9.

brought into being only by a cause necessarily bringing it into being and that what is brought into being is not a cause of its own being, so has Aristotle explained in the *Theology* that the one exists in every multiplicity, because any multiplicity in which the one does not exist would never end.[79] He demonstrates this by clear demonstrations, such as his statement that each part of the multiple is either one or not one. If it is not one, it is inevitably either multiple or nothing. If it is nothing, it results that multiplicity does not come together out of it. And if it is multiple, what then is the difference between it and multiplicity? It would also follow from this that what is infinite is greater than what is infinite.

Then he explains that everything in this world in which the one exists is therefore one in one respect and not one in another respect. [17a] If it is not one in truth but the one exists within it, the one would be other than it and it would be other than the one. He then explains that the true one is what provides oneness to all the rest of the existing things. Then he explains that the multiple is by all means after the one and that the one precedes the multiple. He then explains that every multiplicity that approaches the true one is less multiple than what is at a distance from it, and vice versa.

57. Having introduced these premises, he then ascends to a statement about the corporeal and the spiritual parts of the world. He explains in a salutary manner [a] that they have all been generated by the Creator, may He be glorified and magnified, innovating them and [b] that it is He who is the efficient cause, the true one, [and the] innovator of everything, in the same manner as Plato explains in his books on Lordship, like the *Timaeus* and the *Ablīṭīyā*[80] and in other statements of his. Again, in the books of his *Metaphysics*, Aristotle ascends from necessary demonstrative premises until he makes evident the oneness of the Creator, may His majesty be magnified, in book Lambda.[81] Then he descends, returning to explain

79. See *Timaeus* 27c–29a. That is, it would be infinite. For a discussion similar to what Alfarabi relates here, see *Uthūlūjīyā Arisṭāṭālīs*, ed. Badawī, 134:5–135:11 and 148:5–149:19; see also *Physics*, 8.8.263a4–263b8.

80. It is not clear to what dialogue this is meant to refer. Though the term is somewhat similar to the ones he has used previously to refer to the *Statesman*, *Kitāb al-Būlīṭī al-Ṣaghīr* in section 17 and *Kitāb Būlīṭī* in section 42, there is enough difference to make one doubt that this is the dialogue Alfarabi has in mind. Moreover, the *Statesman* is not normally considered to be a work about lordship.

Persuasive as is Muhsin Mahdi's conjecture that *Ablīṭīyā* renders the Greek title for the Republic, namely, *Politeia*, it fails to account for why Alfarabi also refers to the *Republic* as the *Kitāb al-Siyāsa*; see *Philosophy of Plato*, section 33, note 1.

81. See *Metaphysics*, 12.6.1071b3-8.1074b14 and 9.1074b15-10.1076a3, esp. 7.1072b13-31.

exhaustively how the previous premises are verified—and that in a manner no one before him has surpassed nor anyone after him has achieved, even to our day. Is it then to be presumed that someone with such an approach believes in denying [the existence of] the Artisan and in the eternity of the world?

58. Ammonius[82] has a separate epistle that mentions the arguments of these two sages affirming [the existence of] the Artisan, which we need not present here since it is so well-known. Were it not that the path we are pursuing in this treatise is the middle path—which, were we to eschew it, [17b] we would be like someone who prohibits a moral habit and then practices one like it—we would have spoken at length and said that none of the adherents of the [various] schools, sects, laws,[83] and the rest of the factions has the knowledge about the generation of the world, affirming [the existence of] its Artisan, and giving a summary account of the issue of innovation that Aristotle, Plato before him, and those who pursue their approach have. That is, that all the arguments of the learned in the rest of the schools and sects do not, upon detailed analysis, indicate anything other than the eternity of clay[84] and its perdurance.

If you would like to grasp that, look into the books compiled about "beginnings," the accounts related in them, and the traditions recounted from their predecessors to see marvelous things: one says that at the outset there was water, and it was set in motion; foam gathered from which the earth was constituted; and smoke rose up from which the heavens were arranged.[85] Then [look into] what the Jews, the Magians, and the rest of the nations say, all of which indicates transformations and changes that are contraries of innovation. And [look into] what there is in all their accounts about what will eventually happen to the heavens and the two earths, that is, these two being folded, pulverized,

82. See section 24 and note 26. In "Alfarabi against Philoponus," Muhsin Mahdi indicates that Simplicius, a student of Ammonius the son of Hermias, "mentions this work and explains that it is devoted to proving that Aristotle's god is not merely the final cause of the world but its efficient cause or artificer as well"; see pp. 235–37 and note 9.

83. The term is *sharā'i'*; see note 6.

84. The term is *al-ṭīna* and could also be understood as "matter" or even as "nature." "Clay" seems a better translation here, because it evokes the idea of earth, one of the four elements, and thus suggests that these other learned men did not go very far in their explanations. See also *Quran*, 3:49, 5:110, 6:2, 7:12, 17:61, 23:12, 32:7, 37:11, 38:71, and 38:76.

85. See *Quran*, 11:7, 13:17, and 41:1.

scattered, cast into Hell, and things like that, none of which indicates pure annihilation.[86]

Had God not rescued intelligent and mindful people by means of these two sages and those pursuing their approach, who clarified the issue of innovation by clear and persuasive proofs—namely, that it is making something exist out of nothing; that whatever is brought into being from a certain thing will by all means revert to that thing through corruption; that the world is innovated out of nothing and will thus revert to nothing; and similar signs, proofs, and demonstrations [18a] with which their books are replete, especially those dealing with Lordship and the principles of nature—mankind would have remained in perplexity and bewilderment.[87]

59. We, however, have a method that we pursue in this matter to make it evident that those legal arguments[88] are extremely sound and correct. It is that the Creator, may His majesty be magnified, is the governor of the world. As we explained in our discourse on providence, not even the weight of a mustard seed escapes His attention; nor does any part of the world elude His providence.[89] Indeed, universal providence permeates the particulars; every part of the world and of its conditions is set up in the most appropriate and skillful ways—as the books on anatomy, the uses of bodily organs, and similar natural discourses indicate. And every one of the things of which it is constituted is entrusted to someone who necessarily undertakes it with utmost skill and mastery, reaching from the physical on up to the political, legal, and demonstrative parts. Thus the demonstrative are entrusted to those having clear minds and upright intellects, the political to those having solid opinions, and the legal to those possessing spiritual inspirations. The most general of all these are the legal, and their utterances go beyond the extent of the intellects of those to whom they are addressed. Therefore, they are not blamed for what they are unable to conceptualize.

86. See Genesis, chapters 1–8 and passim; also *Quran*, 14:48, 46:1–6, 82:1–4, 89:21, and 101:4–5.

87. See *Quran*, 28:88.

88. Here, and in the rest of this section, the term is *al-shar'iyya* or *al-shar'iyyāt*; see note 6. For the term "governor of the world" in the next sentence, see *Book of Religion*, section 27.

89. See *Quran*, 21:47 and 31:16.

60. Thus someone who forms a concept of the First Innovator as corporeal and as acting with motion and in time is then not capable of forming a concept in his own mind of something more subtle than that and more suitable for Him. Whenever he conjectures that He is incorporeal [18b] or that He acts without motion, there is no way at all for him to form a concept of it. Were he compelled to do so, his error and straying would increase. He is [thus] excused and is correct in what he conceptualizes and believes. Then [there is] someone whose mind is capable of knowing that He is incorporeal and that His action is without movement, yet is incapable of forming a concept of Him as not being in a spatial location. If he were compelled and obligated to [accept] that, that would lead him to what is worse and more harmful. He, too, is correct in what he believes and excused for what he knows.

61. Similarly,[90] the majority of the multitude is incapable of recognizing [how] a thing is generated from nothing or reverts to nothing through corruption. For this reason, they have been addressed with what they are capable of conceptualizing, perceiving, and understanding. It is, then, not admissible that anything pertaining to that be ascribed to mistake or weakness; rather, it is all proper and upright. For the true methods of demonstration are derived from the philosophers,[91] among whom these two sages—I mean, Plato and Aristotle—are eminent. And the upright, persuasive methods of demonstration are derived from the disciples of the laws who are assisted by kinds of revelation and inspirations.

62. Now for one who has taken this approach and position in elucidating the proofs and setting up the demonstrations for [proving] the oneness of the true Artisan and whose arguments about the manner of innovation and summing up of its meaning are like the arguments of these two sages, it would be reprehensible to presume that corruption has befallen what they believe or that their opinions are disordered.

90. Reading *ka-dhālika,* with all of the manuscripts except the Diyarbekir manuscript, which reads *li-dhālika* ("consequently").

91. Reading *al-falāsifa* with all of the manuscripts except the Diyarbekir and Princeton Garrett manuscripts, which read *hā'ulā'i al-falāsifa* ("these philosophers"). In the next sentence, the term translated as "laws" is *al-sharā'iʿ*; see notes 6 and 83.

[CHAPTER TWELVE: THE FORMS OR DIVINE MODELS]

63. Another instance, also, is the issue of the forms, it being ascribed to Plato that he affirms them [19a] and to Aristotle that he is of a different opinion about them.

64. In many of his statements, Plato points out that existing things have abstract forms in the divine world, and he sometimes calls them "divine models." In the *Ablīṭīyā*[92] there is a discussion indicating that these models neither perish nor undergo corruption, but perdure, and that the ones that do undergo corruption are the existing things that are brought into being.

65. And in the books of Aristotle's *Metaphysics*,[93] there is a discussion reproving those who speak of models and forms that are said to exist independently in the divine world without undergoing corruption. He explains the repugnant things resulting from that. For instance, lines, planes, bodies, stars, and celestial spheres would have to exist there; then movements and rotations for these celestial spheres would [have to] exist. Furthermore, sciences like the science of astronomy and the science of melodies, of harmonic and non-harmonic sounds, of medicine, of geometry, of straight and curved measures, of hot and cold things, and, in general, of active and passive qualities, of universals and particulars, and of matters and forms would [have to] exist there. [These and] other repugnant things articulated in those statements are such that it would take too long to mention here.

Because they are generally known, we can dispense with repeating them here as we have done with the other statements where we pointed them out and where they occur. We will leave any mention of them to anyone who would search them out where they occur and gratify himself by looking into and reflecting upon them. For the purpose we are intent upon in this treatise of ours is to elucidate the method which, if pursued by the seeker after the truth, will not lead him astray but will enable him to grasp the truth aimed at [19b] in the statements of these two sages, without deviating from the right approach to [pursue] what ambiguous utterances cause to be imagined.

92. For the work identified here as *Ablīṭīyā*, see section 57 and note 80. If Alfarabi does have the *Republic* in mind here, he may be referring to discussions of the theory of the forms in the following passages: 5.476a-480a, 6.507a-511e, 7.517a-c, and 10.595b–603e.

93. See *Metaphysics*, 3.2.997a34-998a19.

66. We sometimes find that Aristotle, in his book on Lordship known as the *Theology*, affirms the spiritual forms, explicitly declaring that they exist in the world of Lordship.[94] Taken on their surface, however, these statements inevitably entail one of three [possibilities]: either they are contradictory; or some are Aristotle's while others are not; or they have meanings and interpretations that agree on an inner level while their surface meanings disagree, and they thus correspond to and agree with each other.[95] To presume that despite his proficiency and intense wakefulness and the loftiness of these notions (I mean, the spiritual forms), Aristotle would contradict himself in a single science—namely, the Lordly science—is improbable and reprehensible. And that some are Aristotle's and others not is even more farfetched, since the books articulating those statements are too well-known to presume some to be spurious. It remains, then, that they have interpretations and meanings which, once uncovered, will eliminate doubt and perplexity.

67. Thus we say: since the Creator, may His majesty be magnified, differs in substance and essence from anything else in that He is of a more venerable, more excellent, and higher species, nothing is analogous to, resembles, or is similar to His substance either in truth or metaphorically. Yet, despite this, we cannot avoid describing Him and applying to Him some of these synonymous utterances. It is therefore necessarily requisite for us to know that with each utterance we state as one of His attributes, He remains in essence remote [20a] from the idea we conceptualize from that utterance. For, as we said, He is of a more venerable and higher species. Thus if we say that He exists, we nonetheless know that His existence is unlike the existence of anything subordinate to Him. And if we say He is living, we know that He is living in a more venerable manner than what we know living to be with respect to what is subordinate to Him. Such is the case with all the rest of them [sc., the attributes]. When this idea becomes deep-seated and established in the mind of the student of the philosophy that is beyond physics [sc., metaphysics], it will be easy for him to conceptualize what Plato, Aristotle, and those who pursue their approach have said.

94. Though something like the spiritual forms are affirmed in this work, they are said to belong to the world of intellect; see *Uthūlūjīyā Arisṭāṭālīs*, 159:11–164:2.

95. This ("while their surface . . . each other") is the reading of all the manuscripts except the Diyarbekir and Princeton Garrett manuscripts. These two have the following variant: "and thus correspond to their surface meanings" (*wa taṭābiq ʿind dhālika ẓawāhirahā*).

68. Now let us return to where we took leave of him and say: since God, may He be exalted, is living, willing, and the Innovator of this world with all that is in it, is there any doubt that among the stipulations concerning the living and willing [God] is that He has a concept of what He wills to do and has within Himself the forms of what He wills to carry out? May God be exalted above all similitudes! Moreover, since His essence is perduring, no alteration or change is admissible in Him. And what pertains to His sphere is also perduring and neither perishes nor changes. If the existing things did not have forms and impressions within the essence of the living and willing One who brings into being, what then would He bring into existence and by what pattern would He direct Himself in what He does and innovates? Do you not know that whoever denies this idea with regard to the living, willing Agent must say that what He brings into existence is brought into existence only haphazardly, fatuously, and unintentionally, and that He does not willingly direct Himself toward an intended purpose? This is the ultimate of repugnant things!

69. Hence, it is according to this meaning that you ought to be cognizant of and conceptualize the statements of those sages with respect to what they affirm of the divine forms, not as though they were apparitions subsisting in other places outside this world. For when they are conceptualized according to that approach, [20b] one must assert the existence of innumerable worlds, all of which are similar to this world. The sage Aristotle has already explained in his books on physics what must follow from those who assert the existence of a multiplicity of worlds;[96] and the commentators have elucidated his statements with utmost clarity.

70. One ought to consider this method, which we have frequently mentioned, with respect to arguments about divine matters. It is of great benefit, is reliable in all of this, and neglecting it leads to much harm. In addition, one should know that necessity dictates applying synonymous utterances from physics and logic to those subtle and venerable ideas that are exalted above all descriptions and divergent from all the things that come into being and exist naturally. Even if one were intent upon inventing other utterances and contriving languages other than the ones being used, there would be no approach to utterances from which one could

96. See, *On the Heavens*, 1.8.276a18–9.279b3.

conceptualize anything other than what the senses cling to. Since necessity stands as an obstacle and intervenes between us and that, we limit ourselves to existing utterances, forcing ourselves to bear in mind that the divine meanings we express by means of these utterances are of a more venerable species and are other than we imagine and conceptualize.

71. Plato's statements in the *Timaeus* and in many of his books about the soul and the intellect run the same course, [maintaining] that each belongs to a world different from the other and that those worlds are hierarchical, one higher and one lower, and the rest of what he says similar to that.[97] We must conceive of them in a manner similar to what we mentioned [21a] previously, that is, that by the "world of the intellect" he intends only its sphere and likewise by the "world of the soul," not that the intellect has a location, the soul a location, and the Creator—may He be exalted—a location, some higher and some lower, as is the case with bodies. That is something even beginners in philosophizing would find reprehensible, so how would those trained and schooled in it [assert it]? Indeed, by "higher" and "lower," he means the venerable and superior, not spatial location. And his statement "the world of the intellect" is only the way one says the "world of ignorance," the "world of knowledge," or the "world of the invisible," meaning by that the sphere of each of them.

72. It is the same with what he says about the "overflowing" of the intellect to the soul and the "overflowing" of the soul to nature. By that, he means only the benefit the intellect provides by assisting the soul to retain the universal forms when it apprehends their particulars, by synthesizing them when it apprehends their details and separating them when it apprehends them as collections, by obtaining for it the perishable and corruptible forms lodged in it, and so forth concerning the rest of the ways the intellect assists the soul. By the "overflowing" of the soul to nature, he means the benefit it provides by yearning for what is useful for its subsistence, taking pleasure in it, either insistently or intermittently, and so forth.

73. By the "return of the soul to its world after being released from its prison," he means that the soul, for example, is compelled to aid the natu-

97. See, *Timaeus*, 41d—42d, 44d–45b, and 69e–72d.

ral body in which it resides, and it is as though it yearns for rest. When it returns to its essence, it is as though it were released from a painful prison, to [return to] its own sphere which resembles it and to which it is suited. In this manner, all the other symbols we have not mentioned ought to be measured. [21b] The refinement and subtlety of those ideas prevent them from being expressed in a manner other than that used by the sage Plato and those who pursue his approach.

74. The intellect, as the sage Aristotle has explained in his books about the soul, and similarly Alexander of Aphrodisias and other philosophers, is the most venerable part of the soul. Indeed, it comes into actuality only in the end.[98] By it, divine matters are known, and one becomes cognizant of the Creator, may His majesty be magnified. It is as though it were the closest being to Him in venerability, sublimity, and purity, but not in location. Then the soul follows it, because it is like an intermediary between the intellect and nature, for it possesses natural senses. Thus it is as though it were united at one end with the intellect, which is united with the Creator according to the approach we have mentioned, and at the other end with nature, which follows it in density but not in location.

75. It is according to this approach or according to what is similar, which is difficult to describe in speech, that what Plato says in his statements ought to be known. Indeed, whenever they are taken in this fashion, all doubts and presumptions leading to the statement that there is a difference between him and Aristotle regarding these ideas will disappear. Do you not see that whenever Aristotle wants to explain a certain condition of the soul, the intellect, or Lordship, he becomes circumspect and scrupulous in his speech, which he sets out in the form of riddles and similes? That is in his book known as the *Theology*, where he says:

> Sometimes I am alone with my soul a great deal and I cast off my body and become like an abstract, incorporeal substance. I enter my essence, return to it, [22a] and detach myself from all other things. I am at one and the same time knowledge, the knower, and the known. I see beauty and splendor in my essence such as to bewilder me with amazement. At that moment, I know that I am a minor part of the venerable world and that by

98. The text is very obscure here: *wa annah innamā yaṣīr bi-al-fiʿl bi-ākhirih*. See, however, *De Anima*, 3.4.429a10-430a9, esp. 429a22–24, for an indication of the basic issue.

> my life I am active. When I am sure of this, I let my mind[99] ascend from that world to the divine cause[100] and become as though I were joined to it. Thereupon, light and splendor such that tongues are too dull to describe and ears to hear radiate to me. When I am immersed in that light, reach my limit, and can no longer bear it, I descend to the world of calculation. When I arrive in the world of calculation, calculation conceals that light from me, and at that moment I remember my brother Heraclitus when he commanded seeking and inquiring into the substance of the venerable soul by climbing up to the world of intellect.[101]

This is in a long discussion of his in which, struggling, he wants to explain these sublime meanings, but physical incapacity prevents him from perceiving what surrounds him.

76. Anyone who would like to grasp a little of what he has pointed out—since much of it is difficult and remote—may observe in his own mind what we have mentioned and not chase after utterances in a completely slavish manner. Perhaps he will perceive some of what is intended by those symbols and riddles. They [sc., those who claim that there is a difference between Plato and Aristotle] have exaggerated and struggled; so have those who have come after them in this day of ours and whose intent is not truth but whose objective is prejudice and seeking for faults. They have distorted and altered insistently.[102] Even we—despite great effort, toil, and our complete intention to uncover and elucidate—know that we have attained a very slight amount of what is required, [22b] because in itself the matter is inaccessible.

[CHAPTER THIRTEEN: RECOMPENSE FOR GOOD AND EVIL ACTIONS]

77. Among what it is presumed the two sages Plato and Aristotle hold no opinion about nor believe in is recompense for good and evil actions.

99. Reading *dhihnī*, with the Diyarbekir and Princeton Garrett manuscripts; all the other manuscripts read *dhātī* ("my essence").

100. Reading *al-ʿilla*, with the Diyarbekir and Princeton Garrett manuscripts; all the other manuscripts read *al-ʿālam* ("the world").

101. See *Uthūlūjīyā Arisṭāṭālīs*, 22:2–11 and 23:1–2.

102. Reading *wa lam yaʿdharū*, with the Diyarbekir manuscript; the other manuscripts have *wa lam yaqdirū* ("without success").

78. Yet Aristotle explicitly declares in speech that recompense is necessary by nature. In a letter he wrote to the mother of Alexander [the Great] when the news of his death reached her, and she grieved for him and was resolved to immolate herself, he says:

> God's witnesses on earth—that is, the knowing souls—have all agreed that Alexander the Great is one of the most excellent of the outstanding men of the past. Praiseworthy monuments have been established for him in the central places of the earth and in the extremities of human habitation from East to West. God will surely not bestow upon anyone what He has bestowed upon Alexander the Great except on the basis of preference and choice—and the good human being is the one God has chosen! In some, the signs of having been chosen are manifest; in others, they are concealed. Among those past and present, Alexander the Great is the most well-known for [these] signs: he has the finest reputation, his life is the most praised, and his death is the most flawless. Oh Mother of Alexander, if you are concerned about the great Alexander, out of love for him, do not take on what will distance you from him and do not bring on yourself what will stand between you and him when you meet in the company of the good; strive for what will bring you closer to him—most importantly, take upon your immaculate self the responsibility of making offerings in the temple of Zeus.

Thus, this and what follows in his discourse are a clear sign [23a] that he believed in the necessity of recompense.

79. And Plato has consigned to the end of the Republic the tale articulating the resurrection, standing forth, judgment, justice, scales, and the dispensing of reward and punishment for good and evil deeds.[103]

[CONCLUSION]

80. So, whoever reflects on the statements of these two sages that we have mentioned and then does not swerve to sheer contentiousness will be spared pursuing corrupt presumptions and disordered conjectures and

103. The tale in question is the Myth of Er set down at the very end of the *Republic*, 10.614a-621d.

acquiring the burden of attributing to these virtuous men what they are innocent of and exempt from.

81. With this discussion, we conclude our statement about the harmonization between the two opinions of the two sages, Plato and Aristotle, that we wanted to explain. Praise be to God alone.

Glossary

(ARABIC–ENGLISH)

ALIF

ithār	*preference*
akhīr	*final*
muta'akhkhir	*last*
i'tilāf	*concord*
ta'ammala	*to reflect*
anniyya (also inniyya)	*thatness*
ista'hala	*to deserve*

BĀ'

bukhl	*greed*
bada'a	*to innovate*
badhaḥ	*haughtiness*
tabdhīr	*wastefulness*
bara'a	*to create*
baṣar	*vision*
baṭala	*to nullify*
bighḍa	*hatred*
balagha	*to obtain*
bāla bi	*to keep in mind*

TĀ'

tabi'a	*to succeed*
talā	*to follow*

(ARABIC–ENGLISH)

THĀ'

tharwa	*affluence*
thawāb	*reward*

JĪM

jubn	*cowardice*
jarbadha	*deception*
jarīra	*outrage*
jazā'	*requital*
jaza'	*apprehensiveness*
jalāla	*majesty*
majmū'	*aggregate*
jamīl	*noble*
jumhūr	*public*
tajannub	*avoidance*
jihād	*struggle*

ḤĀ'

maḥabba	*love*
ḥadatha	*to generate*
ḥirṣ	*covetousness*
inḥirāf	*deviation*
ḥasan	*fine*
inḥaṣara	*to be restricted*

(ARABIC–ENGLISH)

ḤĀ' (*cont.*)

haṣala	*to attain, reach*
taḥaffaẓa	*to be heedful*
ḥikma	*wisdom*
ḥumq	*stupidity*
ḥunka	*sophistication*
ḥāza	*to master*
ḥayā'	*modesty*

KHĀ'

khibb	*fraudulence*
khubth	*deceitfulness*
mukhātala	*wiliness*
khasīs	*vile*
khilāf	*difference*
ikhtilāf	*disagreement*
khulq	*moral habit*
khilw min	*devoid of*
khawf	*fear*
khair	*good*
takhyīl	*imaginative evocation*
takhayyul	*imagination*

DĀL

mudabbir	*governor*
dahā'	*cunning*

DHĀL

dhakā'	*quick-wittedness*
dhahl	*absentmindedness*
dhihn	*discernment, mind*

RĀ'

rutba	*rank*
martaba	*ranking*
raḥma	*compassion*

(ARABIC–ENGLISH)

rakhāwa	*slackness*
radī'	*bad*
radhīla	*vice*
taraffuh	*luxury*
riqqat al-nafs	*delicateness of soul*
raḍā	*to content*
riḍan	*contentedness*
irāda	*volition*
tarkīb	*synthesis, combination*
rawiyya	*deliberation*

ZĀY

zawāl	*extinction*

SĪN

sabīl	*approach*
sakhā'	*liberality*
sakhiṭa	*to annoy*
saddada naḥwa	*to aim, direct toward*
sa'ā	*to strive*
maskan	*dwelling*
salaka	*to pursue*
salīm	*unimpaired*
sū'	*wicked*

SHĪN

shajā'a	*courage*
shadda	*to harden, make firm*
sharr	*evil*
sharṭ	*stipulation*
sharīf	*venerable*
ishtirāk al-ism	*homonymity*
sharah	*avidity*
sha'ara bi	*to be attentive*
shaqā'	*misery*
shakl	*shape*
shahwa	*desire*
ishtahā li	*to yearn for*

(ARABIC–ENGLISH)

ashāra bi	*to advise*
tashawwaqa	*to long for*
shawq	*longing*

ṢĀD

ṣaḥīḥ	*sound, healthy*
ṣadda ʿan	*to hinder*
ṣināʿa	*art*
ṣawāb	*correct*
ṣūra	*form*

ḌĀD

ḍabiṭ li-nafsih	*self-restrained*
ḍidd	*contrary*
ḍarb	*type*

ṬĀʾ

ṭabʿ, ṭabīʿa	*nature*
ṭarīq	*method*
ṭalab	*seeking*
ṭamiʿa	*to become ambitious*
aṭāfa bi	*to encompass*

ẒĀʾ

ẓarf	*wittiness*

AYN

istiʿdād	*disposition*
ʿudda	*reserve*
ʿadāla	*justice*
iʿtadal	*to equilibrate, balance*
iʿtidāl	*equilibrium, balance*
ʿadam	*privation*
ʿadam al-iḥsās bi-al-ladhdha	*insensibility to pleasure*
ʿaraḍ	*accident (of the soul)*
ʿiffa	*moderation*
ʿaql	*intellect*

(ARABIC–ENGLISH)

ʿāda	*custom*
ʿāfa	*to feel disgust*
ʿiwaḍ	*recompense*
ʿāʾiq	*impediment*
istaʿāna bi	*to have recourse to*

GHAYN

ghabaṭa	*to admire*
gharaḍ	*purpose*
ghaṣb	*usurpation*
ghaḍab	*anger*
ghamm	*distress*
ghamr	*simple person*
ghāya	*goal*
ghaira	*jealousy*
ghaiẓ	*fury*

FĀʾ

faḥwā	*tenor*
farraqa	*to differentiate*
faziʿa	*to frighten*
tafāsud	*enmity*
faṣl	*differentia*
faṭara	*to endow*
fiʿl	*action*
bi-al-fiʿl	*in actuality*
iftaqara ilā	*to require*
fikr	*calculation*
fahm	*understanding*
tafāwut	*disparity*
afāda	*to provide*
istafāda	*to procure*
fāza bi	*to achieve*

QĀF

qabīḥ	*base*
iqtabasa	*to secure*
muqābil	*opposite*
taqtīr	*stinginess*
iqdām	*boldness*

(ARABIC–ENGLISH)

QĀF (*cont.*)

qaswa	*harshness*
qaṣd	*intention*
iqtaṣara	*to be limited, limit oneself*
iqtanā	*to acquire*
quwwa	*faculty, power*
bi-al-quwwa	*potentially*
qayyim bi-al-nāmūs	*custodian of the law*

KĀF

kadd	*toil*
karāha	*loathing*
iktasaba	*to earn*
kais	*cleverness*

LĀM

iltamasa	*to search*

MĪM

majūn	*impudence*
mādda	*matter*
madīna	*city*
insān madanī	*citizen*
mizāj	*temperament*
makr	*trickery*
malaka (pl. malakāt)	*state of character*
mayyaza	*to distinguish*

NŪN

manḥan	*aim*
nakhwa	*arrogance*
manzal	*household*
manzila	*station*
ansha'a	*to originate*
naqṣ	*defect*
nāla	*to gain*

HĀ'

hadaf	*end*
harab	*fleeing*
inhaḍā	*to inspire*
himma	*endeavor*
tahawwur	*rashness*
istihāna	*contempt*
hawan	*passion*
hai'a	*trait*
hayūlā	*primordial matter*

WĀW

awṣā bi	*to counsel*
tawāḍu'	*respectfulness*
waẓāba 'alā	*to persist in*
waffara	*to augment*
waqāḥa	*insolence*
qiḥḥa	*impertinence*
waqa'a'alā	*to apply to*
waqafa'alā	*to grasp*
tawallā	*to help*
wālī	*helper*
awma'a ilā	*to point out*

YĀ'

yasār	*wealth*
yasīr	*slight, trifling*

ENGLISH–ARABIC

(ENGLISH–ARABIC)

absentmindedness	dhahl
accident (of the soul)	ʿaraḍ
to achieve	fāza bi
to acquire	iqtanā
action	fiʿl
in actuality	bi-al-fiʿl
to admire	ghabaṭa
to advise	ashāra bi
affluence	tharwa
aggregate	majmūʿ
aim	manḥ an
to aim, direct toward	saddada naḥwa
to become ambitious	ṭamiʿa
anger	ghaḍab
to annoy	sakhiṭa
to apply to	waqaʿa ʿalā
apprehensiveness	jazaʿ
approach	sabīl
arrogance	nakhwa
art	ṣināʿa
to attain, reach	haṣala
to be attentive	shaʿara bi
audacity	iqdām
to augment	waffara
avidity	sharah
avoidance	tajannub
bad	radī’
base	qabīḥ
boldness	iqdām
calculation	fikr
state of character	malaka (pl. malakāt)
city	madīna
citizen	insān madanī
cleverness	kais
compassion	raḥma
concord	i’tilāf
contempt	istihāna
to content	raḍā
contentedness	riḍan
contrary	ḍidd
correct	ṣawāb
to counsel	awṣā bi
courage	shajāʿa
covetousness	hirṣ
cowardice	jubn
cunning	dahā’
to create	bara’a
custodian of the law	qayyim bi-al-nāmūs
custom	ʿada
deceitfulness	khubth
defect	naqṣ
deliberation	rawiyya
delicateness of soul	riqqat al-nafs
desire	shahwa
to deserve	ista’hala
deviation	inḥrāf
devoid of	khilw min
difference	khilāf
differentia	faṣl
to differentiate	farraqa
disagreement	ikhtilāf
discernment, mind	dhihn
to feel disgust	ʿāfa
disparity	tafāwut
disposition	istiʿdād
to distinguish	mayyaza
distress	ghamm
dwelling	maskan
to earn	iktasaba
to encompass	aṭfa bi
end	hadaf
endeavor	himma

(ENGLISH–ARABIC)

to endow	*faṭara*
enmity	*taf'sud*
to equilibrate, balance	*iʿtadal*
equilibrium, balance	*iʿtidāl*
evil	*sharr*
extinction	*zawāl*
faculty, power	*quwwa*
potentially	*bi-al-quwwa*
fear	*khawf*
final	*akhīr*
fine	*ḥasan*
fleeing	*harab*
to follow	*talā*
form	*ṣūra*
fraudulence	*khibb*
to frighten	*faziʿa*
fury	*ghaiẓ*
to gain	*nāla*
to generate	*ḥadatha*
goal	*ghāya*
good	*khair*
governor	*mudabbir*
to grasp	*waqafa ʿalā*
greed	*bukhl*
to harden, make firm	*shadda*
harshness	*qaswa*
hatred	*bighḍa*
haughtiness	*badhaḥ*
to be heedful	*taḥaffaẓa*
to help	*tawallā*
helper	*wālī*
to hinder	*ṣadda ʿan*
homonymity	*ishtirāk al-ism*
household	*manzal*
imagination	*takhayyul*
imaginative evocation	*takhyīl*
impediment	*ʿā'iq*
impertinence	*qiḥḥa*
impudence	*majūn*

(ENGLISH–ARABIC)

to innovate	*bada'a*
insensibility to pleasure	*ʿadam al-iḥsās bi-al-ladhdha*
insolence	*waqāḥa*
to inspire	*inhaḍā*
intellect	*ʿaql*
intention	*qaṣd*
jealousy	*ghaira*
justice	*ʿadāla*
to keep in mind	*bāla bi*
last	*muta'akhkhir*
level	*manzila*
liberality	*sakhā'*
to be limited, limit oneself	*iqtaṣara*
loathing	*karāha*
to long for	*tashawwaqa*
longing	*shawq*
love	*maḥabba*
luxury	*taraffuh*
majesty	*jalāla*
to master	*ḥāza*
matter	*mādda*
primordial matter	*hayūlā*
misery	*shaqā'*
method	*ṭarīq*
moderation	*ʿiffa*
modesty	*ḥayā'*
moral habit	*khulq*
nature	*ṭabʿ, ṭabīʿa*
noble	*jamīl*
to nullify	*baṭala*
to obtain	*balagha*
opposite	*muqābil*
to originate	*ansha'a*
outrage	*jarīra*

(ARABIC–ENGLISH)

passion	*hawan*
to persist in	*waẓāba ʿalā*
to point out	*awmaʾa ilā*
power, faculty	*quwwa*
potentially	*bi-al-quwwa*
preference	*īthār*
privation	*ʿadam*
to procure	*istafāda*
to provide	*afāda*
public	*jumhūr*
purpose	*gharaḍ*
to pursue	*salaka*
quick-wittedness	*dhakāʾ*
rank	*rutba*
ranking	*martaba*
rashness	*tahawwur*
reception	*jarbadha*
recompense	*ʿiwaḍ*
to have recourse to	*istaʿāna bi*
to reflect	*taʾammala*
to require	*iftaqara ilā*
requital	*jazāʾ*
reserve	*ʿudda*
respectfulness	*tawāḍuʿ*
to be restricted	*inḥaṣara*
reward	*thawāb*
to search	*iltamasa*
to secure	*iqtabasa*
seeking	*ṭalab*
self-restrained	*dabiṭ li-nafsih*
shape	*shakl*
simple person	*ghamr*
slackness	*rakhāwa*
slight, trifling	*yasīr*

(ARABIC–ENGLISH)

sophistication	*ḥunka*
sound, healthy	*ṣaḥīḥ*
stinginess	*taqtīr*
stipulation	*sharṭ*
to strive	*saʿā*
struggle	*jihād*
stupidity	*ḥumq*
to succeed	*tabiʿa*
synthesis, combination	*tarkīb*
temperament	*mizāj*
tenor	*faḥwā*
thatness	*anniyya (also inniyya)*
toil	*kadd*
trait	*haiʾa*
trickery	*makr*
type	*ḍarb*
understanding	*fahm*
unimpaired	*salīm*
usurpation	*ghaṣb*
venerable	*sharīf*
vice	*radhīla*
vile	*khasīs*
vision	*baṣar*
volition	*irāda*
wastefulness	*tabdhīr*
wealth	*yasār*
wicked	*sūʾ*
wiliness	*mukhātala*
wisdom	*ḥikma*
wittiness	*ẓarf*
to yearn for	*ishtahā li*

Index